The Kingfisher Book of Evolution

The Kingfisher Book of Evolution

Stephen Webster

KINGFISHER
NEW YORK

For Giovanna and Lorenzo
—S. W.

Author Stephen Webster
Consultant Dr. John Brookfield
Editor Jonathan Stroud
Senior Designer Malcolm Parchment
Picture Manager Jane Lambert
Picture Researcher Juliet Duff
Pre-Press Manager Caroline Jackson
DTP Coordinator Nicky Studdart
Indexer Hilary Bird

KINGFISHER
Larousse Kingfisher Chambers Inc.
95 Madison Avenue
New York, New York 10016

First published in 2000

2 4 6 8 10 9 7 5 3 1

1TR/0600/TWP/DIG/150NYM

LIBRARY OF CONGRESS CATALOGING-IN-PUBLICATION DATA
Webster, Stephen, 1957-
The Kingfisher book of evolution/by Stephen Webster.—1st ed.
p. cm.
Summary: Examines the evolution of life on Earth, from the first primitive organisms
to modern humans, and attempts to look into the future.
ISBN 0-7534-5271-5
1. Evolution (Biology)—Juvenile literature. [1. Evolution.] I. Title.
QH367.1 .W43 2000
576.8—dc21   00-027060

Color separations by Digimage, Italy
Printed in Singapore

CONTENTS

△ *Evolution provides a key to the secrets of the past. These fossilized footprints help scientists to calculate the stride length of walking dinosaurs.*

What is Evolution?

The world changes. A hundred million years ago, dinosaurs were the most powerful animals on land, dominating the small mammals. Today, the dinosaurs are gone, and mammals have taken their place. Changes like this have been happening for 3.5 billion years, since life began. At first, all life consisted of microscopic, single-celled organisms. Now there are millions of different multicellular animals and plants covering the globe. Over thousands of years, countless varieties of organisms have appeared, thrived for a while, then vanished, either becoming extinct or changing into new organisms. This ongoing process of life, death, and perpetual change is evolution, and it is the fundamental fact that underpins all life.

Endless varieties

Evolution has created a remarkable variety of organisms. Millions of different species are alive today, all adapted to life in specific environments. Each plant has leaves, flowers, and roots designed to make the most of its habitat, whether it is desert or jungle. Each animal's behavior, coloring, and body structure is precisely suited to its surroundings, too. And because each environment is a little different from every other, evolution has produced a unique range of organisms to fit each one.

Strong similarities

Despite their differences, all animals and plants share many similarities. A zebra on the African plains does not look very different from a horse. Chimpanzees resemble humans in many ways. Birds, with their scaly legs and clawed toes, resemble certain types of dinosaurs. These similarities are a result of evolution. All new species arise from an ancestor. If two species have the same ancestor, they share many traits.

△ *At first glance, the animals crowding around this watering hole seem very different from one another. They actually share more similarities than differences, not least of which is the need for water.*

An elusive idea

Evolution is slow—it has taken millions of years for so many species to develop. Although it can be studied, through fossils and living things, humans took a long time to realize that it even existed. The first person to uncover its secrets was Charles Darwin, 150 years ago.

▷ *The theory of evolution focuses on the extraordinary diversity of life on Earth. It tries to explain how everything—from bacteria to humans—has evolved to look and behave the way it does. It also reveals how every single organism, alive or dead, is part of the great, interconnected web of life.*

The Ancient Greeks

The roots of science, and of evolutionary theory, extend back to ancient Greece. For thousands of years, people used myths—stories of gods and monsters—to explain how the world worked. But during the 500s B.C., Greek thinkers began to discard these myths. They started to observe nature carefully, seeking other explanations. Volcanoes and storms were no longer a sign of angry gods, but the result of impersonal, if still mysterious, forces of nature. Some philosophers dissected animals in order to understand their organs. Others speculated about atoms and the structure of matter. But one of the most important topics the Greeks discussed was the origin and evolution of life.

△ Elephant skulls like this one helped create the myth of the one-eyed giants, the Cyclopes.

Mixed-up monsters

Empedocles (495–435 B.C.) was a Greek philosopher who devised an early evolutionary theory. He believed that mud gave rise to life, and that plants turned into animals. Wondering how the animals got their shapes, he decided that the first creatures were monstrous and deformed: heads were joined to arms, bird wings flapped on their own, and giraffe necks were topped with pelican bills. Yet the combinations kept changing. Over time, the strongest ones survived, and these are the animals we see today.

▽ In Empedocles' theory, the first animals were monsters, built from random body parts. Most died because they could not eat or move. But sometimes, the parts combined in the right way, suitable for life. These animals survived, and are our ancestors.

How myths explained the world

All early cultures had myths—stories of supernatural beings who caused natural events. If a storm drowned a town, for example, an angry god was to blame. The myths also helped explain why animals behave like they do. There are many stories of humans being transformed into a tree or an animal by a god. In Greek mythology, the spider was once a woman who could weave beautiful tapestries. Other stories explained mysteries. The myth of the one-eyed Cyclopes was probably based on fossilized elephant skulls, where the trunk hole looked like an eye. Over time, the myths were replaced by scientific theories.

◁ Arachne was a skillful weaver who insulted the goddess Athena. The furious goddess turned her into a spider. This myth explained why spiders can weave beautiful webs.

Aristotle's view of nature

The philosopher Aristotle (384–322 B.C.) had spent his childhood by the sea and was fascinated by sea urchins, starfish, and mollusks. He insisted that philosophers should watch nature closely and base their theories on their observations. In this he was a forerunner of today's scientists. Aristotle thought that humans are the most perfect of nature's works. He felt that nature had a definite purpose, and that animals existed for the good of people.

▷ Aristotle left many writings about all areas of knowledge. His ideas about the natural world were hugely influential in Europe and the Middle East for almost 2,000 years.

◁ In Aristotle's theory, the purpose of the living world is to benefit people. Fish, for example, exist for humans to eat.

◁ According to the Book of Genesis, God made Adam and Eve and gave them the Garden of Eden. Humans, animals, and plants lived there in perfect harmony. The story presents an ideal vision of how nature should be—ordered, peaceful, and beautiful.

The Age of Christianity

All religions try to explain the beginnings of life and the origins of people. In the West, the most important of these descriptions has been the biblical story of Genesis, which teaches that the world—and all species—was created by God in six days. During the Middle Ages, from A.D. 500 to 1500, the Christian Church grew greatly in strength, persecuting those who disagreed with its message. By the time the first scientists began to study nature, Christian beliefs about the Creation, nature, and humanity's origins were deeply ingrained in the culture.

The Garden of Eden

The biblical story of the Creation, taken literally, says that God made the universe in six days. He finished by creating the first humans—Adam and Eve—and instructing them to live in the idyllic Garden of Eden. This was a place of peace, where Adam and Eve had everything they needed. They were banished from the Garden of Eden when they disobeyed God and ate from the tree of knowledge of good and evil. The story of Eden places humans right at the center of creation—all of nature's riches are given to us to use as we see fit.

▷ Old manuscripts in monasteries and churches often contain pictures of the story of Genesis. These images were greatly admired and helped to make the meaning of the Bible clear. For many hundreds of years, most people in the West got their knowledge about the world only from the Bible, not from scientific experiments.

Noah's ark and the flood

The story of Noah's ark, also from Genesis, demonstrates God's enormous power over nature. In the story, God is shocked by the wickedness of humans, and sends a great flood to kill them. Only Noah's family and a pair of every animal survive aboard the ark. The story of a flood that overwhelms the world was influential for a very long time. Many 19th-century geologists argued that a series of gigantic floods shaped the world's valleys and mountains.

▷ In this picture of the ark, the animals and birds have been saved because of Noah's skill and faith in God. This Bible story implies that people have a responsibility toward all the world's animals.

△ Paley imagined a watch found lying on a beach. Simply by looking at its intricacy, we know that a skillful watchmaker has created it. Christians in the 1700s argued that the perfect adaptation of all life showed that it, too, had been designed—by God.

Proof from design

William Paley (1743–1805) was a theologian who wanted to prove that God existed. He saw that animals and plants were well suited to their environments: fish are streamlined for swimming, and birds have wings and feathers to keep them aloft. Paley argued that this excellent design was proof of a master-craftsman. Just as a good watch can only be made by a skilled watchmaker, so the complex animals around us must have been made by a powerful creator, God.

▷ James Ussher (1561–1656) was Archbishop of Armagh, Ireland, and a great scholar. After closely examining the Bible, he calculated that God created the world on October 23, 4004 B.C. In his day, the Bible was thought to be more reliable than any scientific observations.

Science and the Bible

In the 1600s, the Bible was still unquestioned by most people—Archbishop Ussher used it to calculate that the earth was less than 6,000 years old. Although a few early scientists doubted the literal truth of some Bible stories, it would be centuries before science diverged from religious beliefs. When it did, the effect was huge. Today, scientists believe life has existed for 3.5 *billion* years.

The Rise of Science

During the 1700s, science became a powerful force across Europe. With instruments such as the telescope and the microscope, scientists described worlds that were previously invisible, from millions of new stars in the night sky to tiny bacteria in pond water. Such discoveries, which were widely published, demonstrated that understanding the natural world required observation and experiments. It was now clear that ancient authorities such as the Bible and Aristotle did not have all the answers. Yet, while science and its discoveries became ever more influential, most scientists had no problem believing in both science and God. The thousands of new species of animals and plants discovered simply revealed the magnificence of God's creation.

Great expeditions

The new knowledge depended not only on work in laboratories. Many nations sent explorers to find new lands or precious metals. One of the greatest of these was the German Alexander von Humboldt (1769–1859), who set off in 1799 to explore the waters of the Amazon River in Brazil. With botanist Aimé Bonpland, he collected 60,000 plant specimens. Their accounts of exotic creatures inspired others to earn a living collecting new plants and animals from faraway lands. These were sold to museums, which became treasure houses full of wonders for others to study.

▽ *Bonpland and von Humboldt spent five years gathering data. They traveled over 6,000 miles (9,650 km).*

Geology begins

Large numbers of fossils were unearthed in the 1700s. People found remains of animals that no longer existed and primitive plants preserved as rock. Equipped with hammers and maps, thousands of enthusiasts charted the rocks and tried to understand their structure. These early geologists began to amass evidence that Earth had undergone colossal changes that no one had imagined.

△ *Early fossil finds created great excitement. This giant skull—of an extinct reptile, a* mosasaur—*was found in 1786. It needed several men to lift it. Its size inspired scientists to imagine a lost world full of terrifying creatures.*

Classifying nature

Expeditions returning from the Amazon, Jamaica, Indonesia, and India generated mountains of specimens, many of them completely unknown. At first, there was no system of classification, making it difficult to compare specimens. Carl Linnaeus (1707–1778), a great Swedish scientist, invented a system still in use today. In his book *The System of Nature*, he gave every species two Latin names, the first for the group it belonged to (the genus), the second for the particular organism itself. This "binomial system" made it possible to define relationships between species, showing that each species is unique, but several may be part of the same genus.

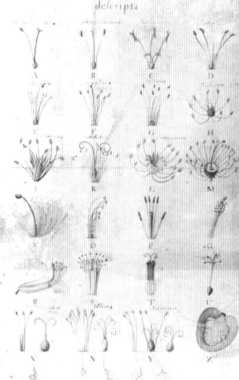

▷ *Linnaeus's system of classification revolutionized the study of nature. For example, he found that he could distinguish plants by examining differences in their sexual organs (the stamens and stigmas).*

Understanding humans

As science advanced, the study of humans progressed, too. For centuries, doctors had relied on ancient texts for traditional cures, rather than investigating the human body. By the 1700s, dissection had become more common, and medical students began to be taught anatomy. Amid a fast-growing tide of discoveries, scientists compared human and animal bodies, and began to notice the many similarities between their structures.

△ *Medical dissection of dead bodies began in the 1500s. Anatomy professors taught students to make accurate observations of organs and limbs.*

Revolutionary Ideas

At the start of the 1800s, scientists began to seriously study fossils. By now, they had gathered specimens from around the world. Meanwhile, naturalists were collecting new species of animals and plants, and giving them to natural history museums and zoos. With so much scientific activity, some surprising new ideas began to emerge. Fossils showed that many animals had become extinct, and that from time to time new ones had appeared. Yet for centuries the Christian Church had taught two basic beliefs about life on Earth. The first was that God created all the world's organisms at once, a theory called "special creation." The second was that the world was very young. These beliefs were disputed by the revolutionary ideas of two brilliant scientists, the French biologist Jean Chevalier de Lamarck and the British geologist Sir Charles Lyell. Their groundbreaking work paved the way for a scientific theory of evolution.

△ *Jean Chevalier de Lamarck (1744–1829) worked in Paris. For years, he studied invertebrates and concluded that they had evolved from one form to another.*

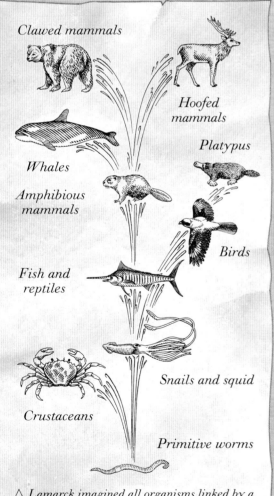

Clawed mammals
Hoofed mammals
Platypus
Whales
Amphibious mammals
Birds
Fish and reptiles
Snails and squid
Crustaceans
Primitive worms

△ *Lamarck imagined all organisms linked by a fountain of life. At the bottom are worms, created from mud. Every organism will evolve up, into more complex and more perfect creatures.*

△ *Lamarck thought that organisms' bodies evolved automatically in response to the environment. At its simplest, this suggests that giraffes evolved by stretching up to eat leaves, each new generation being born with a slightly longer neck.*

Lamarck's breakthrough

Lamarck's theory, published in 1809, was controversial. He explained the similarities between different animals by suggesting that all life sprang originally from primitive worms and had an inner tendency to evolve into more complex organisms. Eventually, this evolutionary force produced mammals and even humans. Lamarck's idea that organisms changed from one type to another is still central to modern theories of evolution. But scientists did not accept his idea that bodily organs change according to how well they fit the environment.

A new approach to nature

As hundreds of amateur scientists helped to classify more and more animals, plants, and fossils, it became increasingly clear that some kind of evolution had taken place. But there was no real evidence for Lamarck's "fountain of nature." The search began for a simpler explanation of evolution. Sir Charles Lyell (1797–1875) came closer to an explanation by providing evidence that the world was considerably older than most people believed.

Secrets of the rocks

In his book, *Principles of Geology* (1830), Lyell showed that the earth was very old. Given time, a river will scour deep into a landscape, changing it over millions of years. Lyell argued that the world is shaped mainly by rivers and "subterranean fire," working slowly over vast lengths of time. With this theory, he challenged the common view that mountains and valleys were made by sudden acts of God. His insight about the earth's age was to have a great influence on Darwin.

▷ *Lyell showed that every geological formation—even awesome canyons—could be created by forces we know today, such as erosion by rivers or the upward push of volcanic heat, provided they took place over millions of years.*

Darwin and the Beagle

Charles Darwin, the British scientist whose ideas shocked the world, was not a very good student. He started out training to be a doctor, but he could not stand dissecting human bodies and hated the operating room, where patients were cut open without anesthesia. So in 1828 he switched careers, moving to Cambridge University to study to become a priest. Once again his teachers were disappointed, and Darwin struggled through his exams. He excelled in just one area—natural history. On long walks through the countryside, he collected many specimens, especially beetles. He knew his talent lay in science, but he still fully expected to be a priest. To his delight, he was saved by a letter from the British Navy inviting him to take part in an around-the-world scientific survey. Darwin accepted the post of ship's naturalist, boarded the HMS *Beagle*, and changed his life forever.

△ *Charles Darwin (1809–1882) is the founder of the modern theory of evolution. On board the* Beagle, *he saw a huge range of wildlife and began to develop his ideas. But he kept his theory secret for many years.*

▽ *The HMS* Beagle *sailed slowly around the world, measuring the depth of the sea and making accurate maps. The captain, Robert Fitzroy, a strict and passionate Christian, was appalled by Darwin's new evolutionary views. Luckily, the two men respected each other and rarely argued.*

A voyage of discovery

Darwin departed from Plymouth, England, in 1831. The *Beagle* was small and cramped, only 100 feet (30 m) long. Darwin was not a good sailor and suffered from constant seasickness, but the voyage had given him new purpose. Now, instead of reading about the jungle, he could explore it in person. The exotic birds and insects he had dreamed about would soon be in his collections. As the *Beagle* sailed across the Atlantic Ocean to South America, Darwin arranged his bottles and nets in his tiny cabin. He was to spend five happy years abroad, observing and collecting.

▽ *On the remote Galapagos Islands, Darwin studied strange creatures found nowhere else on Earth. They included giant tortoises and the marine iguana—a species of large lizard that fed on sea algae and sprawled in huge numbers on the rocky shore.*

A glimpse of evolution

When Darwin set out, he believed in the biblical story of Genesis. Yet, as the *Beagle* crossed the world, he began to change his mind. In South America, he excavated giant fossils of extinct mammals and saw for himself how animals had changed over time. His collections also revealed similarities between animals on separate continents. Had the continents once been closer together? Darwin began to glimpse a constantly changing world.

▷ *On the Galapagos Islands, Darwin observed many species of finches, which had all clearly evolved from a single ancestor.*

A newfound fame

Darwin spent a fair amount of time on land, exploring the geology and the local animals and plants. Back on board, his quarters were too cramped to store his finds. He sent them home in crates to his scientist friends, who opened them eagerly and set to work. Darwin also sent back a journal of his experiences. When he returned to England in 1836, Darwin the naturalist was well known.

△ *Darwin shipped fossils, like this* Toxodon *skull, back to England for study. Large extinct mammals like this proved to Darwin that life on the earth had evolved over time. During the voyage, Darwin's fossils boosted his reputation as a naturalist.*

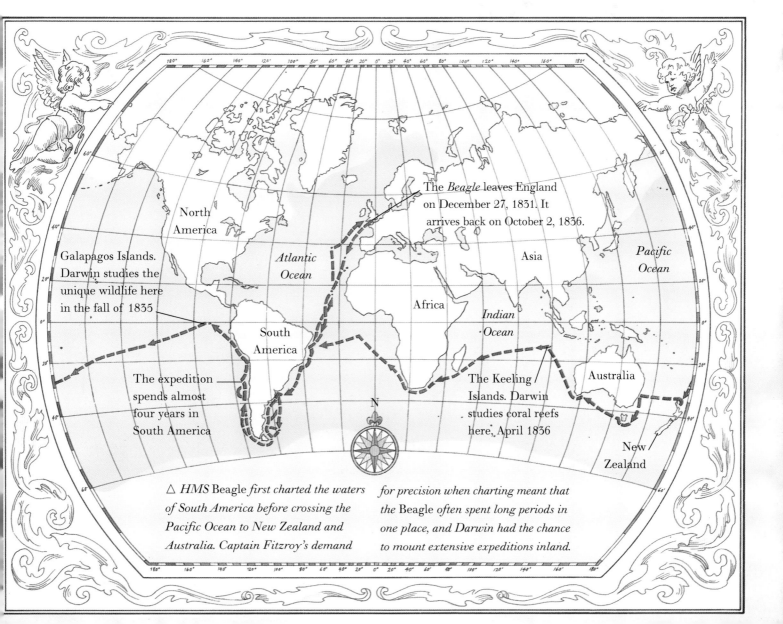

The *Beagle* leaves England on December 27, 1831. It arrives back on October 2, 1836.

Galapagos Islands. Darwin studies the unique wildlife here in the fall of 1835

The expedition spends almost four years in South America

The Keeling Islands. Darwin studies coral reefs here, April 1836

North America

Atlantic Ocean

South America

Africa

Asia

Indian Ocean

Pacific Ocean

Australia

New Zealand

N

△ HMS Beagle *first charted the waters of South America before crossing the Pacific Ocean to New Zealand and Australia. Captain Fitzroy's demand for precision when charting meant that the* Beagle *often spent long periods in one place, and Darwin had the chance to mount extensive expeditions inland.*

The Origin of Species

▽ *For 40 years, Darwin's life revolved around his studies at Down House in Kent, England. His wife, Emma, was a constant support.*

When Charles Darwin returned from his voyage on board the *Beagle*, he immediately set to work on a new theory of evolution. But he kept his ideas secret and instead wrote a book about his travels, becoming famous as an adventurous naturalist. For six years he lived and worked in London, studying his collections of animals and plants and discussing biology with other experts. But Darwin hated life in the city and longed to be surrounded by nature. In 1842 he bought a house in the Kent countryside, where he could work undisturbed. For 16 years he remained there with his wife, Emma, leading a secluded and seemingly uneventful life. Yet all the time, Darwin was putting the finishing touches to a revolutionary theory that would challenge the beliefs of Victorian England.

Life at Down House

Darwin came from a wealthy family, so he did not need a job. Although he suffered a mysterious illness and was often incapacitated by nausea and migraines, he worked incessantly. Darwin's habits never changed. Each day, he wrote letters to naturalists around the world, finding out as much as possible about animals and plants. He also tended to his large collection of pigeons.

◁ *This pouter formed part of Darwin's collection of pigeons. He was fascinated by the dramatic variations between individuals of a single species.*

▷ *Alfred Russel Wallace (1823–1913) was an animal collector working in the Malay Archipelago. While sick with malaria, he conceived a theory of evolution almost identical to Darwin's. They published a joint paper outlining their ideas, but it was Darwin's* Origin *that astonished the world.*

Shared inheritance

Darwin had no doubt that species change over time, but he needed evidence. One vital observation he made was that there are great similarities between different animals —for example, all mammals have hair. Darwin suggested this was because they all evolved from a shared ancestor. Because of evolution, mammal species change, but retain many similarities.

Death and survival

Darwin also avidly studied new ideas. The economist Thomas Malthus had written that human populations are kept in check by disease, famine, and war. Darwin applied this idea to animals and plants. In the wild, many organisms die young, while others survive to old age. Why should this be? Darwin noticed that his pigeons showed huge physical differences, yet were all one species. Here was the key to his theory. The survivors of a species would be the ones with differences that suited their local environment. As environments change over time, the type of survivor changes, too—resulting in evolution.

Publication and outcry

After 15 years of research, Darwin's theory was complete. But still he hesitated to publish it. He feared public reaction to his work and worried that he had missed some crucial facts. But in 1858 he received a letter from Alfred Russel Wallace with the details of Wallace's own theory of evolution. Darwin's friends persuaded him to start writing, and a year later *The Origin of Species* was published. There was so much interest that the book sold out on the first day. Most people accepted Darwin's ideas, persuaded by the amount of evidence he'd collected. But some were angered because they saw no place for God in Darwin's theory.

◁ The Origin of Species *is the most famous work of biology in history. It has convinced many generations that evolution occurs naturally, without supernatural intervention.*

▷ *The idea that humans were part of evolution disturbed many people. Here, a sinister group of apes claims a human child as one of their own.*

After Darwin

When Charles Darwin died in 1882, his theory of evolution had been accepted by scientists and formed the backbone of the growing science of biology. His work not only explained why life on Earth changes, but it also stimulated younger biologists to do research into evolution. As the 1900s progressed, technological advances helped biologists. Electron microscopes revealed the details of cells. Chemical techniques revealed cells' molecules and explained what they did. Outside the laboratory, naturalists combed riverbeds and caves for fossils. Biologists examined the lives of existing animals and plants, and showed how they fit in with their environment. This research has confirmed Darwin's main ideas and strengthened the conclusions he reached.

△ *Like every other animal, humans have evolved. But, unlike other animals, we are able to strongly modify our environment to suit our needs, and often go to great efforts to prolong life.*

The importance of the molecule

From 1950, scientists turned to chemistry for new ways of studying biology. All living things are made of molecules, many of them very complex. The way these molecules contribute to the life of an organism was little understood, but today molecular biology is the main focus of research. The key event in its history was the discovery of the structure of DNA in 1953. Knowledge of the "molecule of life" showed how genetic information can be transmitted from one generation to another. This was a crucial step toward discovering how evolution actually works.

◁ *Francis Crick (1916–) and James Watson (1928–) discovered DNA. The simplicity of the spiral form took biologists by surprise, but led to a revolution in scientists' understanding of inheritance.*

▽ *The film* Inherit the Wind *(1960) dramatized a real-life campaign to ban Darwin's ideas from a classroom in Tennessee.*

◁ *Ecological studies explore how habitats change over time. Scientists have observed how quickly plants recolonize even in devastated areas, such as this lava-covered landscape.*

The broadening reach of science

The late 1900s also saw the development of the science of ecology. With many more scientists working in universities and research stations, far more is known about the everyday lives of animals and plants. The details of adaptation can be closely studied, so that the survival value of an animal's behavior or coat coloration can be better measured. Studies also explore environmental change—a process that is crucial for evolution. Meanwhile, fossil finds have made the history of evolution clearer than ever before. Finds range from human skulls 30,000 years old to 500-million-year-old invertebrate fossils.

Evolution and popular culture

From the beginning, Darwin's ideas have fascinated—and often shocked—the public. To this day, some people refuse to accept them. But popularized ideas about evolution, genetics, and prehistory have poured into novels, comic books, and movies. The science may be inaccurate, but the stories make good use of dinosaurs, mutated monsters, and highly evolved creatures from outer space. Although evolution can be a complex subject, its conclusions are important for everyone. It is extraordinary to think that humans watch movies about dinosaurs, but have themselves evolved from a primitive slime that existed 3.5 billion years ago.

"ONE MILLION YEARS B.C."
RAQUEL WELCH JOHN RICHARDSON
PERCY HERBERT   ROBERT BROWN
MARTINE BESWICK

△ *Movies pitting humans against dinosaurs are completely fictitious. Dinosaurs died out at least 60 million years before humans appeared.*

△ *Science fiction imagines how life might be in the future and speculates where evolution will take the human species.*

▽ *In the movie* Them! *(1954), ants mutate to giant size and begin to terrorize the human population.*

Principles of Heredity

Evolution is hard to study because it happens so slowly. The changes that transform one species into another may take millions of years, but scientific experiments can last only hours or days. In Darwin's time, evidence for evolution could only come from studying fossils and living animals, and, at his death, an important problem remained unsolved. This concerned heredity—how information is passed between generations. One of the basic truths about organisms is that offspring are similar to their parents. Giraffes only make giraffes, not zebras. Yet, over time, descendants do begin to differ from their ancestors, so eventually a new species forms. Why does this happen? Scientists now know that the answer lies within the tiny genes hidden in every cell. Evolution occurs because genetic information is passed down through the generations and changes slightly along the way. This process is called "inheritance" and is studied by geneticists.

Chromosome

△ *Humans have 23 pairs of chromosomes. Each person's sex is determined by the sex chromosomes, X and Y. Females are XX, males are XY.*

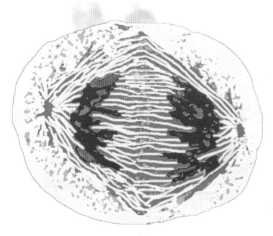

△ *Chromosomes (in red) are only visible during cell division, when the DNA that makes them is twisted into a tight spiral to take up less space.*

Into the cell

Every cell in an animal or plant contains a nucleus, the control center that contains the cell's genetic information. Using powerful microscopes, early geneticists began to study the chromosomes—structures inside the nucleus that are visible when the cell divides. During cell division, chromosomes reproduce themselves. Scientists realized that this was the way material was passed from one generation to the next, but they still did not know what chromosomes contained.

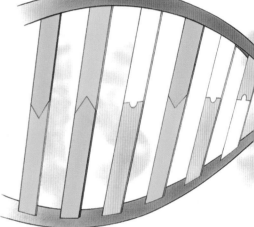

△ *The cross-spokes of the DNA molecule consist of four base chemicals—adenine, thymine, cytosine, and guanine. Their order along the molecule forms the genetic code.*

The structure of DNA

The molecule inside chromosomes that seemed to hold the key to inheritance was DNA (deoxyribonucleic acid), but it took scientists until 1953 to discover its shape and how it worked. Each chromosome contains a long, folded strip of DNA. Built like a twisted ladder, its inner structure is composed of four smaller molecules—adenine, thymine, cytosine, and guanine. The arrangement of these chemical bases along the length of the DNA forms a code, or set of instructions, that stores information about the organism. Every DNA strip is split into sections called genes, each of which has a specific task in the animal or plant.

Radiation damages DNA

▽ *A chromosome is made of DNA twisted around groups of protein molecules called histones. The total length of DNA in a cell may be several yards, so the chromosome's neat packaging is vital.*

◁ *DNA has a self-repairing mechanism that limits the number of changes that pass to the next generation. But radiation and chemicals can damage the molecule, change the order of the chemical bases, and thus alter the proteins. Some mutations are harmful and hinder the organism's survival; some changes are helpful and so become widespread in the population.*

Histones

▷ *After cell division, chromosomes untwist, and the DNA floats freely in the nucleus. This makes it easier for the cell machinery to access the code.*

The key to change

For evolutionists, DNA is fascinating. It stores information about an organism and copies itself each time a cell divides. Since DNA is almost the only material that passes from adult to offspring, any similarity between generations relies on DNA. Yet DNA is also responsible for the *changes* that occur between generations. Changes to DNA are called mutations—tiny areas of damage to its molecule, perhaps caused by radiation. If changes occur in the reproduction cells, mutations will be passed to the next generation. They may be very tiny, but enough of them could form a new species. If DNA did not change, there would be no evolution.

The code for building the body

If DNA just carried information, it would be useless. But it is valuable because each organism's cells take the information from the DNA and use it to make another group of important molecules. These are the proteins that are used to build cells and organs and to regulate the body's chemistry. But first, DNA has to be decoded, and this is a highly intricate process. It starts in the cell's nucleus, where the DNA code is copied and then sent out into the body of the cell. Here, special manufacturing zones, or ribosomes, take charge. They use the code to build the proteins, which are then set to work.

◁ *Proteins are made of strings of smaller molecules called amino acids. The DNA gives information about which amino acids should be used, and in what order. In the human body, there are thousands of proteins, each built from 20 types of amino acids.*

Variation

△ *Gregor Mendel (1822–1884) is the founder of genetics. He was a monk who used his monastery garden to set up revolutionary experiments investigating inheritance in peas.*

The theory of evolution tries to explain why animals and plants have so many shapes and sizes. From soft-bodied worms to colossal whales, there is a seemingly endless variety of life, all of which is a result of evolution. However, there is another kind of variation that allows evolution to happen. It is the variation that exists among animals and plants of the same species. When any population is examined, something remarkable is found—there are genetic differences between each individual. These differences mean that within a herd of zebras, for example, each animal looks and behaves differently from the others. This variation stems from sexual reproduction.

▷ *Meiosis is the mechanism that ensures variation in all sex cells—and thus in all offspring. Chromosomes pair up to mix genetic information before splitting again.*

1 *2* *3* *4*

◁ *At the moment of fertilization, the egg's and sperm's chromosomes combine to give the new organism a unique genetic makeup.*

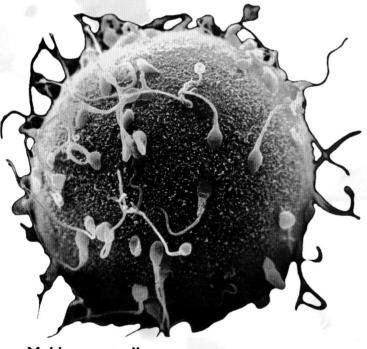

Making sex cells

Before sexual reproduction takes place, the male's sperm and the female's eggs are made by a special kind of cell division, called meiosis. Pairs of a cell's chromosomes line up, interlink, and swap sections of DNA. This produces brand-new combinations of genes in the new cells.

How meiosis works

At the start of meiosis, all the chromosomes in the cell pair up. Each chromosome copies itself exactly, so there are four strands in each pairing (1). The strands then mingle and interlink (2). Then, sections of chromosomes are swapped, mixing the DNA information they contain (3). The chromosomes then separate into pairs again (4) and then split off on their own. Finally, each one joins chromosomes from other pairs in four new sex cells (5). This process means that each new sex cell has a unique combination of genes.

Fertilization

All sexually-reproducing organisms begin life with fertilization. This is the instant when the chromosomes in the egg fuse with those of the sperm, forming a new cell, the zygote. Fertilization is possible because both parents have the same number of chromosomes, so the chromosomes can form pairs. With its paired chromosomes, the zygote will grow into a unique individual. But its survival and chances of reproduction will be strongly influenced by the genes that it happens to have.

△ *The variation within this population of people is caused partly by genes and partly by environment. Intelligence, weight, height, and skin color are each a mixture of environmental and genetic influences.*

◁ *The land snail shows a great range of shell patterns. Studies indicate that the patterns are effective in camouflage, and that each one suits its environment, from grassland to forest.*

How variation leads to evolution

Most environments change slowly. In any population, some organisms will be better adapted than others to new conditions because of the genetic variation they have inherited. These well-adapted organisms are most likely to have the most offspring. Thus, the gene combinations that produce these extra adaptations are passed on to more offspring than other combinations. If the environment keeps changing and these combinations are still favored, a new species eventually forms.

Non-genetic variation

Some variation is not caused by genetics. When plants get a good supply of water and nutrients, they will grow taller and stronger. This variation is caused by the environment and will not be passed on to the next generation. In every population, some variation is because of the environment, and some because of inheritance. Like all organisms, humans vary, but for important features, such as intelligence and personality, it is impossible to distinguish the genetic influence from the environmental.

◁ *The natural selection of variation leads to evolution. This zebra, fleeing the lioness, may escape because of a combination of genes that gives it greater speed. By surviving longer, the zebra is more likely to pass on its favorable genes, which in time will become more and more common.*

5

Population

When Charles Darwin investigated animal and plant populations, he knew that for the population of a species to stay level, each couple should produce only two offspring. But he saw that some organisms usually produce a much higher number—insects lay hundreds of eggs, birds can lay six or more eggs in a single clutch, and plants produce seeds by the thousands. Some animals are even more spectacular—a cod may spawn a million eggs. Despite these numbers, it is rare for populations to rise suddenly. In nature, they usually stay roughly level, as though each mating pair does bring up just two offspring in the end. So although every population of organisms has the potential to increase exponentially, they rarely do so. This insight gave Darwin a vital clue.

◁ *Dandelions produce hundreds of seeds, but few will germinate and reach maturity.*

▽ *If all the offspring of all plants and animals survived to adulthood, the world would quickly become extremely crowded.*

◁ *The bloodsucking hookworm lives in human intestines, clinging to the bowel wall with hooklike teeth. Disease-causing parasites like this are just one of the factors that control a population's numbers.*

Population and death

Darwin realized that there must be a tremendous death rate among animal young, with very few offspring becoming adults. When the cod releases her eggs, the vast majority are eaten or destroyed. Even birds, with attentive parental care, suffer many casualties—fledglings may starve, be eaten, or simply fall from the nest. Parasites also attack animals and plants, either killing them outright or weakening them, making them less likely to survive. For Darwin, this explained the steady populations. But then he began to wonder about which of the offspring are most likely to die.

Genetic variation and population

In a sexually-reproducing population, all offspring differ. There are countless variations in body form and strength. Darwin did not know what caused these differences, but today we know that some of them are caused by genes. Some differences may make certain offspring more likely to survive into adulthood. In a family of young zebras, some may be better at fighting off infection. If they run at slightly different speeds, it is the slowest that is most likely to be killed by predators. So the deaths among organisms are not random. It is the weaker and less well-adapted that are least likely to grow up to have their own young.

△ *Natural variations in climate can control a population. The need for water is basic, and when drought strikes, the death toll is heavy.*

▷ *Predators, like this eagle, control other populations by killing a proportion of each generation. If the number of small mammals increases, the extra food leads to a rise in the numbers of birds of prey, which in turn curb the mammal population.*

Thomas Malthus

Darwin's ideas were influenced by a book about human population by the economist Thomas Malthus (1766–1834). Malthus saw that populations could grow much faster than any possible increase in agricultural yield. This meant that only the resulting famine, disease, and war would control the human population. Darwin took this idea and applied it to nature.

Natural selection

Darwin saw that a large proportion of each generation dies. Less successful variants are picked off by predators or disease. For Darwin, this selection of a few was the mechanism of evolution. He called it "natural selection." There will always be pressure on any population of organisms. There is never enough food or space, and the demands of the environment change constantly. In each generation, a population will lose its less well-adapted members, while the better-adapted ones will flourish and pass on helpful characteristics to their young.

◁ *In the 1800s in England, good sanitation and housing were rare, and people lived in very crowded conditions. Malthus argued that such overcrowding was only controlled by famine and disease.*

△ *This camouflaged stick insect is adapted for sitting on plants. However, for any adaptation to work, the animal's behavior is as important as its shape and color. A stick insect that chose to sit on a flower head would not camouflage at all.*

Adaptation

Every living organism is suited to its environment. This fit between the design of an organism and its habitat is called "adaptation." Adaptation is extremely precise—for example, a stick insect's camouflage only works on the right plant. In the past, such precision was considered proof of God's existence. But evolution gives a simpler explanation. Chance genetic variation guarantees that some individuals fit the environment better than others. They will survive because they are more likely to find food or fend off predators. This process—natural selection—favors well-adapted organisms and spreads their genes through the population.

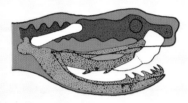

△ *In pythons, the vertebrate skeleton is adapted to allow an enormously enlarged jaw. The jaw hinge is mobile and swings down to make the throat big enough to swallow large prey.*

Adaptations of the skeleton

All vertebrates have a bony inner skeleton that performs the same function—it supports the animal's body. Yet skeletons vary greatly, too, so that each species has its own finely adapted version. Skeletons first evolved in fish over 450 million years ago. Since then, some fish have evolved into land animals and birds, so the basic design has changed to deal with life on land or in the air. Each change, from the development of a snake's jaw to a rabbit's strong hind legs for running, shows natural selection in action.

▷ *With a highly muscular esophagus and stomach, this snake is adapted to swallow its prey whole.*

Feeding adaptations

No organism can survive without a well-adapted feeding system. Feeding adaptations are not only found in the teeth, jaws, stomachs, and enzymes. Behavior is vital, too, so that an animal can hunt its prey or sense a far-off watering hole. Any individual that by chance inherits poorer feeding skills is likely to die before reproducing. In each generation, it is the individuals with the best skills that pass on their genes. Over time, environments change. If they become drier, the best-adapted animals may be able to survive drought. Those adapted to a wetter climate may not survive.

▷ *The body tissues of desert animals are adapted to cope with severe dehydration. The fat in a camel's hump can provide water and nutrients for several days— they can survive conditions that would quickly kill a human.*

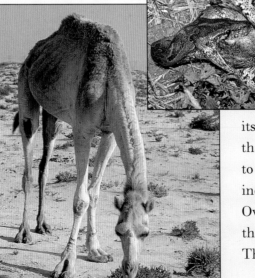

Sensory adaptations

All animals and plants are sensitive. They respond to sound and light, and even to magnetic fields. Such sensitivity is vital for safe movement, for finding food or a mate, and for communication. As a result, some of the most remarkable adaptations involve brains and eyes, antennae and feelers. Every environment makes different demands upon a sensory system, and no badly equipped organism could survive. Animals that travel by night must steer by smell or by echolocation— a form of radar. Green plants do not have eyes, but they must sense light, which is vital for their growth. Their leaves are adapted so that they can turn to collect the most light, and even grow toward it.

△ *A moth's antennae detect even a few scattered molecules of pheromones, or sex scent. They also absorb radar signals sent out by bats to avoid this predator.*

△ *The 20-foot (6-m)-long great white shark is superbly adapted for streamlined movement in water. Its teeth, powerful muscles, and acute sense of smell—which can detect a particle of blood across great distances—are all adapted for the shark's predatory habits.*

▽ *Vultures are not adapted for killing, but for scavenging. Their bald necks keep them from getting caked with rotting blood.*

Locomotion

All animals need to be adapted for travel in their environment. Moving through water is much harder than moving through the air, so fish need to be streamlined. Water supports fish against the pull of gravity, so their bones can be fairly light. By contrast, land animals need bones strong enough to lift their body off the ground as they move. Birds have to overcome gravity altogether to fly, and their adaptations emphasize strength and lightness. Their bones are hollow, but strong enough to support the muscles attached to them.

Endless change

Most environments change over time, so adaptations will change, too, because what works in one environment may not work in another. But natural selection can only modify, it cannot invent. The organism's basic structure is always present, even in the most elaborate adaptation.

The Formation of New Species

In the 3.5 billion years of life on Earth, countless new species have evolved, existed for a time, then disappeared. Although many species share certain characteristics and may appear similar, each is different from any other species that has ever lived. They are all unique—from *Tyrannosaurus rex* to the bumblebee. The appearance of each new group is a response by living things to specific changes in their environment. The exact circumstances that produce a group can never be repeated, and once a species becomes extinct, or evolves into another species altogether, it is lost and will never appear again. Charles Darwin's theory of evolution showed how species can change, and his insights still provide a valuable guide to the fabulous variety of living things on Earth.

△ *The Tasmanian wolf was a marsupial that evolved into a wolflike shape. It died out in the 1930s.*

What is a species?

On one level, a species is simply a group of organisms that are very similar. So the species "puffin" is a group of birds common in the North Atlantic. Puffins breed in burrows on land and possess the same multicolored bill, orange feet, and comical walk. Descriptions like this are useful, but evolutionists have a much simpler way of sorting organisms into species: two organisms are considered part of the same species if they can mate together and produce offspring. Puffins mate with other puffins, but not with other related birds, such as razorbills or common murres. Therefore, these birds belong to separate species.

▽ *In this imaginary example of speciation, a group of deerlike mammals roams freely on a plain. They are one species and interbreed easily. The gene flow through the population ensures that the animals all look almost identical.*

▷ *Gradually, a mountain range rises, and the population is split. The animals cannot cross the range, and breeding between the two groups ceases. Rainclouds do not pass the mountains, and the environment on the far side becomes a desert.*

Making new species—reproductive isolation

One important way that new species evolve is by speciation —by splitting an old group. The remote Galapagos Islands have several species of finches. Scientists believe that a few million years ago, a group of finches from South America were blown onto one island and settled there. Later, a smaller group flew onto another island. The two groups were now reproductively isolated on separate islands. Over thousands of years, the groups adapted to their islands, becoming different species with their own genetic makeup. This happened so many times that new species of finches were formed.

How many species?

No one knows how many species there are on Earth. So far, 1.4 million species have been identified—of these, 750,000 are insects, 250,000 are plants, and 41,000 are vertebrates. But there are probably many more, mostly insects hidden in the world's remaining rain forests. One biologist found 3,000 species of insects in a single tropical tree, and estimated that there may be 30 million other insect species alive. But time is running out—many species are becoming extinct even before they can be recorded.

△ *The Galapagos Islands were colonized by organisms from the mainland. Each island now has a unique collection of species.*

◁ *The woodpecker finch and the cactus finch are two of the 14 species of Galapagos finch. Each one has evolved a different size and shape of beak.*

Convergent evolution

Each new species must be adapted to its environment. As a result, unrelated species evolving in similar environments may look almost the same. The Tasmanian wolf looked a lot like a dog, but it was a marsupial that had exploited the same carnivorous lifestyle as dogs and wolves.

▷ *Over millions of years, the isolated groups adapt to the new conditions. The desert animals evolve new traits, such as a pale coat to reflect heat and large ears to help heat loss. If the two groups met now, they could not interbreed. They are separate species.*

The Evolution of Sex

Sex is a biological mystery. It is a part of reproduction, but only the females in a species can produce offspring. Half of the species—the males—cannot produce young at all. This is a surprise, because according to Darwin's theory of evolution, a successful species must try to produce as many young as possible. If maximizing numbers is the priority, then asexual reproduction is a much better method. In it, there are no sexes—every member produces offspring. Yet sexual reproduction seems favored in nature. From bacteria to humans, sex is a fact of life.

△ *Aphids are capable of both sexual and asexual reproduction. In good conditions, every aphid is female, and produces young without being fertilized. As a result, aphid populations can rise very rapidly.*

△ *Even the simplest organisms have sex. These two paramecia have united to exchange genetic material. Evidence like this suggests sex evolved in primitive organisms early in the history of life.*

What is sex?

Sex simply means that an animal or plant exists in two mating types—male and female—with both forms needed for reproduction. When sexual reproduction takes place, both sexes contribute an equal amount of genetic material, which passes on to the next generation. An important feature of sex is that each sex usually makes an unequal contribution. The males contribute genetic material, but—at least at first—not much else. The females, however, contribute not only genetic material, but also the means of making and nurturing eggs. Even today, biologists find it hard to explain how such an inefficient system could evolve. Why is it worthwhile to have only half the population able to produce young?

The advantages of sex

When males and females prepare their genes for the next generation, they package them in special cells called gametes. The production of gametes involves remixing a parent's genes, and when the female gamete (egg) is fertilized by the male gamete (sperm), more genetic mixing occurs. The resulting genetic variation spreads through the population and has important advantages. It may result in protection against parasites, which are a threat to most organisms. And crucially, in the long term, variation allows a species to evolve as the environment changes.

△ *Parasites, such as mosquitoes, are a burden to other organisms and have influenced evolution for millions of years. Sex can produce new generations that may be immune to the parasites.*

Finding a match

Sexual reproduction is the union of two sets of genes. Fertilization is successful if the genes match—usually from individuals of the same species. Genes are packaged into chromosomes. Only half the original number of chromosomes goes into any gamete. During fertilization, chromosomes are restored to their original number, with each gamete contributing an equal number. Different species cannot match up their gametes because their chromosome number may not be the same and their genes may be arranged differently.

◁ *Sometimes, members of two different species are closely related enough for fertilization. As with this "tiglon"—half tiger, half lion—the offspring of such a mating is likely to be infertile.*

The roles of males and females

Though males neither make eggs nor provide the first nourishment for developing embryos, they often have a role in nurturing the young. The existence of two sexes can therefore be an advantage, allowing a division of labor, with males and females taking different roles. Every species has evolved its own pattern of male and female behavior, designed to maximize sexual reproduction. In some species, males mate with more than one female; in others, monogamous relationships are the norm. Chimpanzees are often promiscuous, while birds are known for sexual loyalty.

◁ *The existence of two sexes can lead to markedly different roles for each. In this gorilla family, the giant father offers protection while the mother tends the baby.*

Sexual versus asexual reproduction

The result of sexual reproduction is that the new generation is never an exact copy of the old. Each time reproduction takes place, the parents' genes are mixed, leading to offspring that are entirely unique. This makes it more likely that the new generation will cope with the demands of a changing environment. Many animals and plants use a simpler form of reproduction—asexual reproduction—in which each parent produces identical copies of itself. Because each individual can reproduce, the population can grow quickly. The disadvantage is that the new generation will not be able to deal any better with environmental changes than the old.

▽ *Males are essential for sexual reproduction, but their role after fertilization varies. In the case of the black widow spider, for example, the female eats the male once his sperm has fertilized her eggs.*

Evidence of Evolution

I t is impossible to directly observe and measure the evolution of new animals and plants—the process happens much too slowly. So scientists need other means of gathering information about how life changes. Since Darwin's time, the most important method has been to study rocks and fossils. They can be used to reconstruct events that occurred millions of years ago, to imagine how ancient animals behaved, and even to figure out what the climate was like then. It is a difficult task—fossils are easily destroyed over millions of years, but each surviving fragment contributes a small piece to the story. Alongside this amazing visual record of the evolution of life, today's scientists can now also get a huge amount of information from experiments in genetics and ecology. At the beginning of the twenty-first century, evidence of evolution is flooding in from every area of biology.

△ *John T. Scopes (1900–1970) was a biology teacher in Tennessee whose lessons about evolution led to his prosecution for blasphemy in 1925. He was fined $100.*

Creationism

Not everyone agrees that biologists are correct. For example, fundamentalist Christians, or creationists, do not believe the theory of evolution. They believe that the Book of Genesis in the Bible is the only source of information about the origin of life and of people. Creationists oppose the idea that species can evolve, and do not regard fossils as evidence of evolution. Creationists believe that humans were created by God, not that humans evolved from apes by natural selection over million of years.

Fossil evidence

Scientists use fossils to provide unique glimpses into the past. However, fossil records are only a patchy guide to the lives of extinct animals and plants. Only the hard parts of an organism tend to be fossilized. When an animal dies, the internal organs quickly decompose or are eaten, leaving only the bones to turn into rock. Even bones only fossilize if they are buried in exactly the right way. And if a fossil does form, it can easily be destroyed by rock movement or volcanic action. Finally, most fossils remain buried too deep to be discovered by scientists.

△ *An animal will only fossilize under the right conditions. A fish dies and sinks (1). Its flesh decays, but the skeleton is buried before it is damaged (2). Protected under the sand, the skeleton slowly changes into rock (3) and emerges later when its rock stratum is exposed (4).*

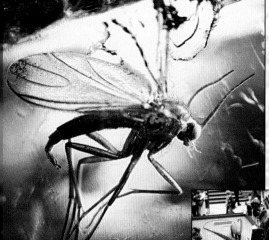

Preserved bodies

Stone fossils are not the only form of preservation. Insects do not decay if they are caught in the leaking sap of pine trees. Amber, often used in jewelry, is formed from drops of sap that have hardened over millions of years. Insects trapped inside for 50 million years or more are easy to examine. Sometimes their body chemicals can be extracted. Whole-body preservation can also occur if an animal dies and is buried in ice or a tar pit and remains undisturbed. Mammoths, frozen for 10,000 years, are sometimes discovered in Siberia. They must be carefully thawed out before their skin, body organs, and even their DNA are examined.

◁ *An insect preserved in amber is revealed in exquisite detail. If the internal organs and arteries are preserved, chemicals such as DNA can be extracted.*

◁ *Fossil discoveries are not only of interest to scientists. Fossil dinosaurs at natural history museums across the world draw huge crowds. Their bones provide a vivid reminder of a lost age.*

The "living fossil"

Occasionally, an extinct animal is found to be still alive. In 1938, an unusual fish was caught off the coast of South Africa. It was a coelacanth—a fish believed to have been extinct for more than 80 million years. The coelacanth was already famous as a close relative of the first fish that crawled onto land. Scientists filmed it and noticed that it used its fins in a walking motion similar to that of a land animal. This "living fossil" thus provided evidence of the first amphibian.

Continental drift

Organisms evolve because their habitats change. Mountains rise and fall. Jungles are submerged by seas. These changes take a long time and are largely caused by the drifting continents. The crust of the earth is broken into segments, called tectonic plates. Heat from deep inside the earth slowly drives these plates around. As they move, continents and oceans change size and position, altering the climate. By studying continental drift, scientists gain insights into how evolution took place in the past.

△ *The coelacanth was thought to be extinct, but was found alive and well off the African coast. It has thick, fleshy fins, similar to those of the fish that first crawled up onto the land, and which became ancestors to all of the land vertebrates of today.*

▷ *These three diagrams show the position of the world's continents in the Triassic (1), early Jurassic (2), and early Cretaceous (3) periods. Scientists study rocks and fossils to reconstruct these maps of Earth millions of years ago.*

1   2   3

New Techniques

Modern science does not rely solely on fossils for studying evolution. When organisms evolve, it is not only their appearance that changes. Deep inside the cell, the genes change, too. The alterations are tiny, but can be observed in a laboratory. Protein molecules made by the genes also change, and these changes can be glimpsed by scientists as they occur. It is now known that the basic cell machinery of all organisms is the same, so experiments on a bacterium can give useful information on the evolution of elephants, or even humans. Modern biology can thus perform experiments in evolution by examining the minute chemical reactions that happen in every cell.

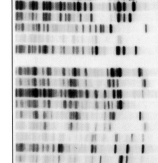

◁△ *Scientists can record any individual's DNA as a unique pattern (left). Comparing the DNA of different species allows us to identify pairs of species, such as humans and orangutans, which are genetically similar.*

The importance of DNA

Genes are made of DNA, the molecule that gives the cell information on how to grow and link up with other cells. Genes are involved in the day-to-day running of cells as well as the structure and behavior of the entire organism. All organisms rely on DNA and genes, so this system of cell control must have evolved early and been inherited by every organism.

Comparing DNA

Because all organisms use the same system of genes and DNA, they are easily compared. Scientists can check the DNA of a chimpanzee and find out how different it is from the DNA of a human. The two are very similar— about 99 percent the same. Although a chimp and a human look and behave very differently, they share most of their evolutionary history. Even a bacterium and a human share many genes, but the more closely two organisms are related, the more similar their DNA is.

Artificial mutation

Over 3.5 billion years, the mutation of genes has been a constant source of variation. Without variation, evolution cannot happen, so mutation is an important part of the history of life. Yet most gene mutations are harmful and make an organism less well adapted. Scientists can now make mutations by exposing organisms to chemicals or X rays. By watching mutations move through several generations of flies, scientists create a laboratory version of evolution that helps reveal how the process works.

◁ *Genes in this* Drosophila *fruit fly have been artificially mutated. Where antennae should be, extra eyes now grow. These mutations will be inherited, so their passage through the laboratory's fly population can be studied.*

Microscopic evidence

Powerful microscopes have revealed tiny structures, called organelles, in cells. One of them, the mitochondrion, strongly resembles a bacterium. It even has its own DNA, slightly different from that of the cell. The mitochondrion converts food into the chemical energy needed for life. Some scientists think that cells didn't evolve mitochondria, but just "swallowed" bacteria that were good at releasing energy. The theory is called "symbiosis," which means "living together."

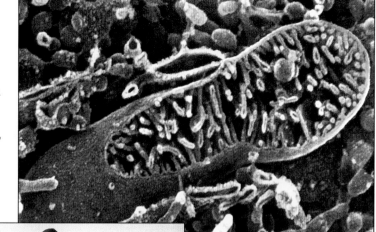

▷ *Ice dug out in the Antarctic contains bubbles of air thousands of years old. These ice cores give evolutionists information about the history of Earth's atmosphere.*

△ *This mitochondrion has an important role—to provide energy for its cell. It resembles a bacterium, and has its own DNA. According to the symbiosis theory, mitochondria were once free-living, but were swallowed to help cells get energy.*

The peppered moth

Sometimes, when an environment changes unusually fast, evidence can be found of a population of animals evolving. The peppered moth exists in dark and light forms, both eaten by birds. Surveys show that when a landscape is polluted, and the tree trunks are blackened with soot, the dark moth is more common. If pollution decreases, and the trees lighten, more pale moths survive. The population alters because birds eat more of the badly camouflaged, and thus badly adapted, moths.

An ongoing task

The modern theory of evolution is based on research carried out using a wide range of sophisticated techniques. Biologists have to gather evidence and continually update evolutionary theory. There will always be arguments about the details, but as time goes on, the evidence for evolution will grow as well.

◁▽ *In Britain in the 1800s, industrial pollution from new factories began to cover many trees in soot. This made the previously common, pale form of the peppered moth dangerously visible and easy prey. In contrast, the rarer dark form flourished.*

How Life Began

The story of evolution starts long before planet Earth was formed. Ever since the universe began, exploding stars have scattered atoms throughout space. Sometimes these condense into solid planets and burning stars. Earth formed from this dust 4.5 billion years ago. For a billion years, it spun around the sun, hot and devoid of life. It collided with giant asteroids, melting the land and turning the oceans to steam. Lightning and radiation from the sun made cyanide, which rained into the seas. It was a hellish, poisonous world—yet these conditions led to life.

△ Meteorites often contain chemicals important for life, including carbon. The space debris that showered the early Earth may have been a vital raw material for the first simple life forms.

▽ Today's simplest cells, like these blue-green algae, can survive without oxygen. They are descendants of Earth's earliest cells. However, the first life forms must have been simpler still, perhaps lacking a surface membrane or even DNA.

▽ Life arose 3.5 billion years ago. The temperatures were similar to today's, but volcanoes and lightning made the planet a violent, uninhabitable place. Yet these conditions were vital for life. Only later, once algae had released oxygen into the air, did the atmosphere resemble our own.

The early atmosphere

At first Earth's atmosphere contained no oxygen. Few modern organisms can survive without oxygen, which is used to release energy from food. For life to begin, however, a lack of oxygen was vital. Oxygen is reactive. It combines with other atoms and changes them—it would have destroyed the first delicate cells. Instead of oxygen, the early atmosphere was filled with unreactive gases, which protected early life and gave it a chance to survive.

△ American chemist Stanley Miller (1930–) made amino acids with early atmospheric gases—like carbon dioxide, methane, and ammonia—and a spark.

Early life

No one is certain how life began, but life's most important molecules contain carbon. At first, carbon molecules were probably concentrated together on the edges of oceans and tidal pools, or even on ice or lumps of clay. Then chemical reactions in the sea or atmosphere over thousands of years made the first life forms. These life forms were probably simple. They may have been fatty bubbles floating in water, able to absorb molecules and divide in two.

The experiments of Stanley Miller

In 1953 Stanley Miller, a student at the University of Chicago, collected in a bottle the gases he thought covered the early Earth. He simulated the violent atmosphere of the time by sparking electrodes inside the bottle. After a few days, he found a brown smear inside. In it were amino acids—carbon molecules needed by living things. Miller had shown how a few molecules essential to life might have formed on Earth. But this was not the same as creating life.

△ *On the ocean floor, hot vents spew out minerals from under ground. Colonies of bacteria live beside these vents, providing nourishment for a food chain of organisms that never see daylight. Some scientists speculate that life may have originated around such vents, or even under ground.*

△ *Trilobites were early arthropods. They lived on the seabed, crawling over the sand. As they walked, their spiny legs dislodged tiny particles of food, which were propelled forward into their mouths.*

Life in the Sea

For almost 3 billion years after it first appeared, most life consisted of single-celled organisms drifting in the seas. Then, in a sudden flurry of evolutionary activity 550 million years ago, the first complex animals appeared—the invertebrates. At first they were all soft-bodied. Some were filter feeders, sifting food in the water. Many, similar to today's jellyfish, trapped organisms as they floated in the current. Then some animals developed shells or hard, jointed limbs. These early mollusks and arthropods were more mobile and better armed than other animals. An arms race began, with species evolving to catch or avoid others. By 400 million years ago, fish—the first animals with backbones—were masters of the seas.

Hunting and surviving

Invertebrates evolved many defenses to keep themselves safe from attack. Ammonites withdrew into their shells; jointed arthropods, such as trilobites, curled up in a ball or used their legs to scuttle to safety. For a time, some arthropods became the sea's top predators. Giant water scorpions grew to over 6 feet (2 m) long and were armed with vicious claws. Their supremacy was short-lived— fish were quickly evolving a more formidable weapon.

▽▷ *By the Devonian Period (395–346 million years ago), the oceans were teeming with life, from sponges, anemones, and mollusks to sharks and giant armored fish.*

▷ Acanthodes *was an early jawed fish. Its body was protected by scales and sharp spines.*

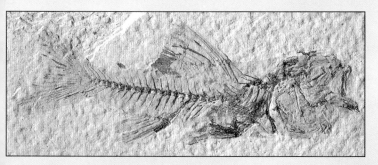

△ *Bony fish have strong, flexible skeletons. They also possess air-filled swim bladders that allow them to adjust their buoyancy, and rise or sink.*

The evolution of jaws

The first fish, the agnathans, had no jaws—their round mouths could only suck in specks of food and water. They had a bony outer casing, and a tail and fins for swimming. Then, about 410 million years ago, some fish began to develop jaws, made out of the bones of their gill arches. These were a revolutionary weapon. As muscles and teeth developed, and jaws became both movable and powerful, jawed fish quickly began to dominate the oceans.

Sharks and bony fish

Jawed fish soon developed streamlined bodies and sharp senses, and could move swiftly through the seas in search of food. Among the first were the sharks. Their skeletons were made of soft cartilage, which supported a long and muscular tail that powered the sharks through the water. Other fish developed bony skeletons and thin, delicate fins, which were extremely maneuverable. These fish still dominate the seas today.

◁△ Dunkleosteus *was a colossal jawed fish, over 30 feet (10 m) long. Its huge jaws were filled with sharp, stabbing bone plates, which allowed it to devour any other creature—even early sharks.*

▽ *Mollusks, such as ammonites, used their air-filled shells for buoyancy as well as protection.*

◁ *The lamprey, a modern descendant of the agnathans, has no jaws, only a simple mouth to attach itself to the body of its prey and suck their blood.*

▽ *Belemnites were mollusks with conical shells, related to octopuses and squid.*

◁ Stethacanthus (bottom), *a 28-inch (70-cm)-long shark, had a strange, anvil-shaped dorsal fin. Scientists believe this may have been used to attract a mate.*

Out of the Water

About 450 million years ago, the first life appeared on land. Until then, all organisms had lived in the oceans and rivers. Water environments hold many advantages for living things. They are not subject to extreme temperature changes. Water also protects its inhabitants from the full force of gravity and keeps them buoyant. Simple organisms, like jellyfish, can float through water, but in the air they are weighed down and immobile. Most important, life forms living in water will not dry out. Many organisms are 90 percent water, so to dry out is to die. But the otherwise hostile land held one big attraction—there were no predators. The pioneers who finally took advantage of this were those who could avoid drying out and could cope with gravity's pull.

▷ The primitive liverwort lives in damp conditions because it needs water to reproduce. The male sex cells swim toward the female sex cells, and they unite. Then a stalk grows up, able to spread spores over a wide area of ground.

The first land plants

The first primitive plants to appear on land were wholly dependent on a moist environment. Liverworts and mosses, which still thrive today, lived in places saturated by ground water. To reproduce, they relied on sex cells swimming from leaf to leaf, and on sealed spores able to resist drought. They did not try to overcome gravity, but grew horizontally, hugging the ground. This strategy was effective in watery places, but plants could only invade the land completely when they were able to grow tall and conserve water. This breakthrough came with the evolution of woody stems, which provided support and a way of carrying water from the ground up to the leaves.

△ Ferns evolved woody stems, able to hold the leafy fronds freely in the air. Height is an advantage for a plant, because it can reach into the light. Yet ferns still depend on water for reproduction, so they are usually found in damp conditions.

▷ Giant water scorpions as much as 6.5 feet (2 m) long were the dominant predators at this time.

The invertebrate invasion

Invertebrates quickly followed plants. Spiders, mites, and springtails, less than half an inch (1 cm) long, clambered over the topsoil, living off the remains of dead plants or off each other. They were well adapted to the new conditions. Their strong, jointed limbs were able to resist gravity, and their hard outer skeletons were sealed and waxy, to keep body water in.

△ *Arthropods flourished on land. As with this modern millipede, a waxy cuticle and a jointed skeleton prevented drying and aided movement.*

Plants grow upward

Ferns were the first plants able to rise free from the soil. Their tough, woody stems contained a system of tiny pipes that drew water up to the leaves. Yet even ferns needed water to help them reproduce, because their sex cells meet only by swimming. Later, plants evolved the system of pollination, whereby air and insects carry the sex cells. In this way, plants reduced their dependence on water and invaded the driest terrain.

▷ Trigonotarbids, *early relatives of spiders, were only 0.02 inches (0.5 mm) long!*

Vertebrates on Land

▽ *Acanthostega lived 365 million years ago. Although very fishlike, it had four strong legs.*

When plants and invertebrates began to live on land, soil started to form from their remains. The soil's nutrients washed into rivers and estuaries, encouraging fish out of the oceans and into shallow fresh water. Finally, during the Devonian Period, around 380 million years ago, some fish crawled onto dry land. They left behind a watery habitat full of dangerous predators, but on land there was a huge supply of food and no predators. There were reasons to stay on land, but perhaps these adventurous fish could only survive for a few hours before having to head back into the water. Yet their experiment was a success, and it paved the way for the first amphibians.

◁ *The fish that came on land had fleshy fins, strengthened by a few bones and firmly attached by muscle to the main skeleton. In time, these limbs evolved into the arm and leg bones of the amphibians.*

Adventurous fish

Some bony fish had evolved primitive lungs from their air-filled swim bladders. This allowed them to take gulps of air if there was little oxygen in the water. But only a few had firm, muscular fins, strong enough to pull their body out of the water. The fins were probably clumsy, but they had many advantages—the fish could find new food, and even survive drought if the stream dried up. Over time, these four weak fins would become the arms and legs of all four-legged vertebrates.

Fish's fleshy fin, supported by strong bones

Hind leg of an early amphibian, showing how the fish's bones have evolved

Amphibians appear

The fish that crawled on land evolved into the group of vertebrates called amphibians, represented today by frogs and newts. One was *Acanthostega*, which had true arms and legs rather than just fins. Surprisingly, each arm ended not with five fingers, but eight. *Acanthostega* was fishlike, too, with a tail for swimming, and it continued to use gills to breathe as well as lungs. It probably spent most of its time in the water, but vertebrate groups that needed water only for drinking would soon evolve.

▷ *The modern lungfish is related to the first fish to crawl on land. It can move overland on fragile legs and can cocoon itself in mud to survive drought.*

◁▽ *The mammallike reptiles* Edaphosaurus *and* Dimetrodon *both had giant sailfins. These controlled the temperature of their blood, allowing them to absorb heat from the sun, or to release it if they grew too hot. By trapping heat efficiently, both predator and prey could get the energy to move fast—to chase and to escape!*

△ *The herbivore* Edaphosaurus *had large, crushing teeth to grind tough vegetation. It is known as a "sailback" because of its spiny vertebrae, covered by a web of skin.*

◁△ Dimetrodon *was a large and fierce carnivore, able to hunt animals its own size. It was at least 10 feet (3 m) long and very heavy.* Dimetrodon *was able to lift its body away from the ground and race after its prey.*

▷ *Reptile eggs were vital for the conquest of land, because they did not have to be laid in water. Inside its shell, the egg contains enough water and food to let an embryo grow into a hatchling able to survive on land. The egg is porous, taking oxygen in and releasing waste carbon dioxide. Eggs protect the embryo well, making it more likely to survive.*

The first reptiles

Reptiles evolved from amphibians and were the first vertebrates to truly conquer the land. They had a dry, waterproof skin, efficient lungs for breathing air, and, most important, they could lay eggs far from water. Their skeleton had evolved, too, so their bodies were lifted slightly above the ground. Without the friction caused by crawling, reptiles could move much faster. Then, around 300 million years ago, a new group evolved, the mammallike reptiles. With specialized teeth able to cut meat, crush seeds, or grind vegetation, these new reptiles soon dominated many land habitats.

45

The Dinosaurs

Around 225 million years ago, a new group of reptiles became the dominant land animals on Earth. They were the dinosaurs, and they remained the most numerous, varied, and successful group of species for a staggering 160 million years. According to the theory of evolution, such long-lasting success can only be explained as a result of good adaptation. If dinosaurs were clumsy, stupid animals, as they have often been portrayed, they could never have lasted so long. Instead, they must have been intelligent and sociable, able to adapt and survive in a wide range of conditions.

◁ Allosaurus *was a Jurassic carnivore, up to 40 feet (12 m) in length. Like the later* Tyrannosaurus rex, *its front legs were relatively weak, and it probably relied on teeth the size and shape of steak knives to fatally wound its prey. Its 3-foot (90-cm)-long skull had large holes in it to help reduce its weight.*

△ *The herbivore* Triceratops *was the size of a rhinoceros. It may have used its enormous horns for defense or in mating displays.*

▷ *The giant herbivore* Barosaurus *lived about 150 million years ago, in the Jurassic Period. Weighing a colossal 60 tons, it most likely used its 30-foot (9-m)-long neck to graze constantly on tree foliage.* Barosaurus *was too large to be threatened by the small carnivorous dinosaur* Ornitholestes. *Only 6 feet (2 m) long, but fast and agile,* Ornitholestes *probably hunted lizards and early mammals with its powerful, grasping claws.*

A clue to the dinosaurs' success

Unlike ordinary reptiles, whose legs spread out on both sides of their bodies, dinosaurs had legs like pillars, directly under the body. They efficiently supported the body's weight. Many dinosaurs even became bipedal, standing only on their hind feet. This skill has led some biologists to argue that, like mammals, dinosaurs were homeothermic—able to maintain a constant, warm body temperature. Good balance is needed to be bipedal, and only a centrally-heated, lively brain can work fast enough to provide the necessary stream of instructions.

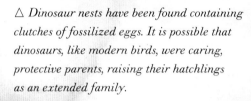

△ *Dinosaur nests have been found containing clutches of fossilized eggs. It is possible that dinosaurs, like modern birds, were caring, protective parents, raising their hatchlings as an extended family.*

King of the carnivores

There were many shapes and sizes of dinosaurs, from the giant herbivores, such as *Barosaurus* and *Diplodocus*, to insect-eating carnivores the size of chickens. Best known are the large, bipedal carnivores. The largest of these, *Tyrannosaurus rex*, evolved about 70 million years ago, shortly before the dinosaurs became extinct. Its colossal 3-foot (1-m)-long skull was powerfully built to withstand the massive impact as it lunged at its prey. It had small, clawed arms, but probably relied on the initial biting attack to kill its victim.

The extinction

Around 65 million years ago, the dinosaurs suddenly became extinct. Many other animals also perished at this time. Scientists have long wondered how the dinosaurs could disappear so quickly, after such a long period on Earth. One argument is over the speed of the extinction. No one knows whether dinosaurs disappeared in the space of one year—or over 300,000 years. Fossils suggest that they were already in decline, perhaps because of slow climatic changes, when a giant meteorite hit Earth and accelerated their destruction.

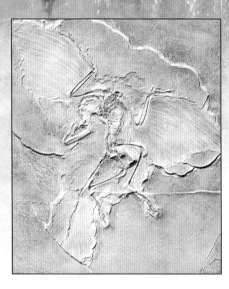

△ Archaeopteryx *is a Jurassic fossil with bird and reptile features. It had feathers, like a bird, but it still retained the teeth and long, bony tail common in reptiles.*

Life in the Air

To crawl along the ground, a land animal has to overcome the force of gravity. The skeleton and muscles work to move it along. When an animal flies through the air, however, the difficulties are greater. The animal has to be light, but with wings large enough to give the body lift. A sophisticated nervous system is also needed to direct the wing muscles and ensure a safe landing. When animals evolve and overcome these obstacles, a flying animal has many advantages: it can easily search for food, land-based predators are less threatening, and if the environment deteriorates, a flying animal can look for an alternative habitat. Today, birds and insects reveal the advantages of flight.

◁ A cricket has two sets of wings powered by muscles inside the thorax. It takes flight using its strong jumping legs.

Archaeopteryx

One of the world's most famous fossils is *Archaeopteryx*. With teeth and feathers, it seems to be halfway between a reptile and a bird. It was the size of a small crow and probably was able to fly. *Archaeopteryx*, the oldest known bird, is thought to have evolved from a dinosaur. This discovery led some scientists to view birds as descendants of dinosaurs.

▷ The flying lizard's ribcage extends to serve as a wing that it uses to glide.

Ancient insects

Long before the evolution of pterosaurs and birds, insects were already airborne. The first great forests, which flourished 300 million years ago, were home to many flying insects. The largest, *Meganeura*, looked like a dragonfly. It had a wingspan of 28 inches (70 cm).

◁ Ornithocheirus (foreground), a coastal pterosaur from the Cretaceous Period with a 40-foot (12-m) wingspan, glided over the ocean like a modern albatross. Behind it, the pterosaur Tapejara and some early birds crowd the cliffs.

▷ A golden eagle displays the modern bird's mastery of flight. With superb eyesight, it looks for prey from high above and swoops down for the kill with claws outstretched. The wings are adapted for soaring, but also maintain a controlled dive.

The flying reptiles

The first flying vertebrates were the flying reptiles, or pterosaurs. They evolved alongside the dinosaurs, about 130 million years ago, and were skilled flyers, with wingspans up to 50 feet (15 m) across. Pterosaurs took off by jumping from trees or cliffs. Their wings were made of skin stretched tight along the forearm. The hollow wing bones were light, but strong enough to beat to the contractions of the massive pectoral muscles.

Today's masters of the air

There are 9,000 species of modern bird. All are warm-blooded, which allows their brain and muscles to act quickly. Their bones are light, but it is their feathers that give the birds their superb flying skills. Feathers cover the wings and give them a precise, aerodynamic shape. Therefore, the wings can provide lift even when the bird is just gliding. When the bird plunges or turns in the air, the feathers are strong enough to bear the stress.

Mammals

Over the last 65 million years, mammals have become the dominant life forms on Earth. Their first feature is variety—they range in size from blue whales to the tiny pygmy shrew. Their second is adaptability—different mammals have evolved to dominate every habitat from arctic snows to deserts. Others have successfully taken to life in the sea and air. This dramatic success is based on certain mammalian traits. All mammals are intelligent creatures, good parents, and very sociable, but their most important feature is that they are homeothermic—their blood temperature is controlled internally and is always hot. The constant warmth has allowed the evolution of a big, active brain and fast-acting, reliable muscles.

△ Megazostrodon, *an early mammal living in Africa 220 million years ago, probably ate worms, insects, and dinosaur eggs.*

△ *The rare duck-billed platypus is a monotreme, a primitive mammal that lays eggs and secretes milk through the skin instead of through teats.*

▽ Thylacosmilus, *a fanged marsupial predator, evolved a shape similar to the placental saber-toothed tigers.*

Types of mammals

Today, there are three types of mammals. Monotremes are the most primitive. Although they are hairy and warm-blooded, they lay eggs like reptiles. Marsupials, such as the kangaroos of Australia, form the second group. They bear live young, but then nourish the baby in a pouch for a long time. The most successful mammals are the placentals, the group to which humans belong. Placentals are born well developed, are suckled by the mother, and have sophisticated teeth.

▷ *Over 10 feet (3 m) long,* Toxodon *was as big as a rhinoceros. It ate grass and foliage, and had a thick hide to protect itself from predators.*

The age of mammals

The first mammals evolved about 225 million years ago from reptile ancestors. At first they remained small and ratlike; it was only when the dinosaurs died out that mammals were able to replace the reptiles as the most populous animals on Earth. Before long, they became the dominant life forms on land. As this scene from South America one million years ago shows, mammals rivaled the dinosaurs in size, variety, and bizarre form.

△ *Tigers show all the features that have made mammals so successful. The large skull houses an intelligent brain, strong jaw muscles, and teeth adapted for killing. Good parental care also maximizes the cubs' chances of survival.*

▷ Megatherium *was a giant sloth 16 feet (5 m) tall. It was probably hunted to extinction by humans only 11,000 years ago.*

▷ *Mammals' teeth differ according to their diet. This elephant's tooth has sharp ridges for grinding vegetation.*

▽ Glyptodon *was slow and cumbersome, but was protected from predators by its heavy armor.*

The importance of mammals

Humans think of mammals as the most "advanced" animal group—intelligent, warm-blooded, and successful. Perhaps we see it this way because we are mammals, too. In evolutionary terms, mammals have been around for only a short time. We have a long way to go to match the success and staying power of creatures such as bacteria, invertebrates, or fish.

The Whole Story

Because of fossils, studies of living organisms, and DNA analysis, a great deal of evidence has been collected about the history of life. But it is the theory of evolution that helps make sense of this evidence and allows a clear picture to be drawn. The theory explains why organisms have so many similarities. If outwardly different organisms, such as birds and reptiles, share a distant ancestor, they probably share many structural characteristics. Yet the theory of evolution also reveals why organisms are *different*. Life on Earth is so old that small genetic differences gradually accumulate, masking the similarities, and leading to millions of different species.

(((Segmented muscles

▬ Nerve cord

Notochord (stiffening rod)

Pharynx

Digestive system

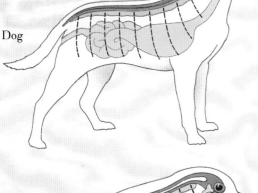

Dog

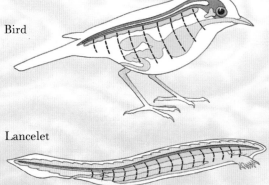

Bird

Lancelet

△ *Vertebrates, such as dogs and birds, still display the basic body structures found in the primitive, 2-inch (5-cm)-long lancelet, a cephalochordate. The lancelet is probably very similar to the common ancestor of all vertebrates, including humans.*

Cnida
(e.g. sea anemon

Fungi

Bryophytes
(e.g. liverworts)

Psilophytes
(the first land plants)

Clubmosses

Horsetails

Ferns

Gymnosperms
(e.g. conifers)

Angiosperms
(e.g. all flowering plants)

Quaternary

Tertiary

Cretaceous

Jurassic

Triassic

Permian

Carboniferous

Devonian

Silurian

Ordovician

Cambrian

Cenozoic

Mesozoic

Paleozoic

Similarity and difference

The tree of life shows when groups of organisms arose, and gives the basic relationships between them. For example, both mammals and birds can be traced back to reptiles. Ancient ancestral links can be seen, too. All living vertebrates, including mammals, birds, reptiles, and fish, are surprisingly closely related to sea urchins and primitive marine organisms such as the lancelet, which do not have backbones. Comparing their body plans shows that all these creatures share basic features, including a central nerve cord. Darwin's theory of natural selection explains how evolution has continually modified the basic structures, with each organism adapting them to different habitats and lifestyles. The existence of these basic patterns is strong evidence for evolution, and indicates how the structures of ancient common ancestors are preserved over time.

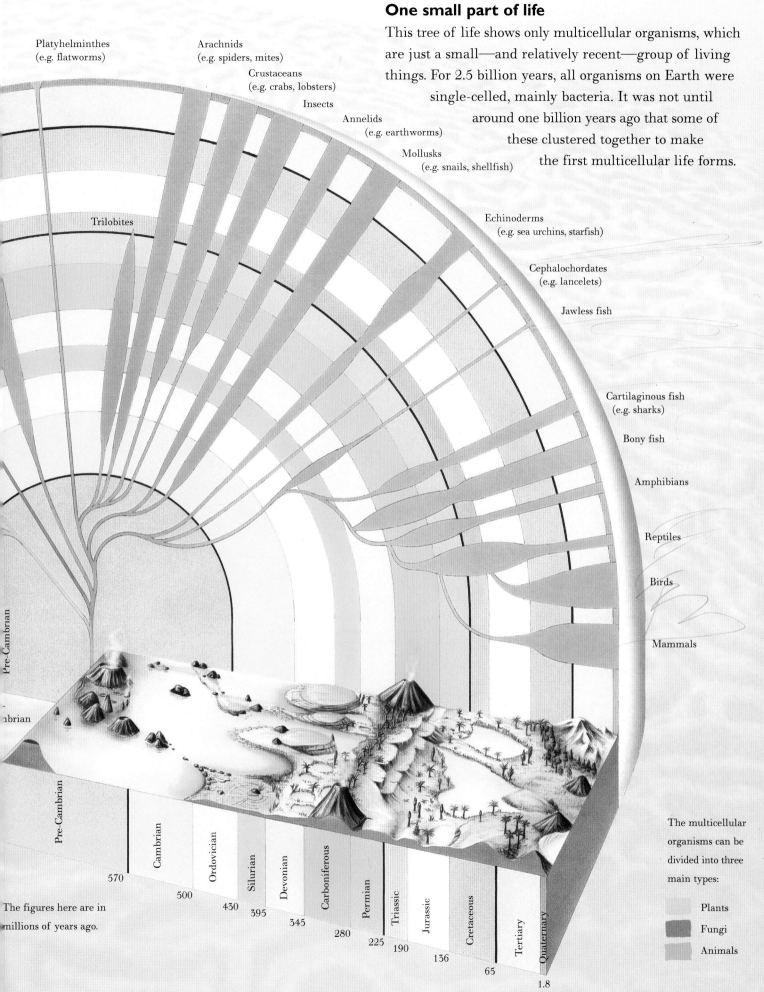

Platyhelminthes
(e.g. flatworms)

Arachnids
(e.g. spiders, mites)

Crustaceans
(e.g. crabs, lobsters)

Insects

Annelids
(e.g. earthworms)

Mollusks
(e.g. snails, shellfish)

Trilobites

One small part of life

This tree of life shows only multicellular organisms, which are just a small—and relatively recent—group of living things. For 2.5 billion years, all organisms on Earth were single-celled, mainly bacteria. It was not until around one billion years ago that some of these clustered together to make the first multicellular life forms.

Echinoderms
(e.g. sea urchins, starfish)

Cephalochordates
(e.g. lancelets)

Jawless fish

Cartilaginous fish
(e.g. sharks)

Bony fish

Amphibians

Reptiles

Birds

Mammals

Pre-Cambrian

Pre-Cambrian

Cambrian

Ordovician

Silurian

Devonian

Carboniferous

Permian

Triassic

Jurassic

Cretaceous

Tertiary

Quaternary

570

500

430

395

345

280

225

190

136

65

1.8

The figures here are in millions of years ago.

The multicellular organisms can be divided into three main types:

Plants

Fungi

Animals

53

Cooperation

If survival and reproduction are the aims of every organism, every animal and plant should constantly be struggling to do better than its neighbor. To a great extent, organisms do show this fierce individualism, such as when they fight for a mate. Yet animals frequently work together, and may even put themselves in danger to help another's chances of survival. This behavior, called "altruism," seems to contradict Darwin, but actually makes sound evolutionary sense. Most examples of cooperation involve organisms that are genetically related, sharing up to 50 percent of their genes. Helping out your relatives might be risky, but it increases the likelihood of your genes being passed on to the next generation.

△ *The tiny tussock bird cleans parasites from the elephant seal's skin. The bird gets a meal, while the seal is restored to health. Even though they are not genetically related, both animals benefit, and their chances of survival are increased.*

◁ *A close, cooperative relationship has evolved between this cleaner fish and the larger labroides cod. The cleaner fish finds a ready meal, while the cod's scales are cleaned of parasites.*

▽ *Wood ants farm aphids for the honeydew that the aphids produce as they feed. In return, the aphids are protected from predators.*

Cooperation between species

Shared genes cannot explain why animals from different species sometimes help each other. Such relationships are examples of reciprocal altruism, in which each animal benefits from the other's altruistic behavior. For example, cleaner fish are often found in the company of large sharks. The cleaner fish picks dangerous parasitic crustaceans off the shark's skin. In return, it gets not only a guaranteed meal, but also the shark's protection from other predators. According to Darwin's theory, such behavior evolved because both animals benefit.

△ *In an amazing example of cooperation among social insects, some honeypot ants have developed into living storage vessels. They hang from the ceiling and are fed with nectar collected by other ants in the colony until their bodies are huge and swollen. When food is scarce, the other ants tickle them, forcing them to regurgitate the precious load.*

Social insects

Insects such as ants, bees, and termites have evolved an extreme form of cooperation. These animals live in huge colonies with each individual fixed rigidly in one role. There is one queen, whose job is simply to produce millions of eggs. The mainly female workers do not breed, but work to bring food, repair the colony, or fend off enemies. A few males exist simply to fertilize the queen's eggs, and then die. Although most individuals do not breed, they are all so closely related to one another that most of their genes are passed on through the queen. In effect, the colony functions as a single superorganism.

Dividing jobs

Cooperation often evolves to protect the safety of every member of the group. African meerkats live in social colonies of 20 to 30 animals. The meerkats divide up their work, so that some members of the colony keep watch for danger, while others guard the young. Even genetically unrelated meerkats will benefit from the enhanced security of the settlement. Such division of labor is also common among many types of insects, where size and appearance depend on an individual's job. Leaf-cutter ants come in two sizes—large ones carry leaf pieces back to the nest, while small ones ride on the leaves and fend off parasites.

△ *Meerkats from the Kalahari Desert in southern Africa use teamwork to survive when foraging outdoors. The ground is open and exposed, but each member of the group participates in keeping watch for danger. They also team up to feed their young.*

Building a colony

A key advantage of cooperation among social animals is the workforce that can be amassed to construct a nest. Termites construct massive mounds up to 25 feet (8 m) tall, carefully designed with vents and shafts for efficient ventilation. The extraordinary naked mole rat, a desert mammal, has evolved an organization similar to that of these social insects. Only 4 inches (10 cm) long, mole rats work to construct enormous tunnel systems, which can stretch up to 2 miles (3 km), sheltering them from the harsh sunlight, snakes, and other threats.

▽ *Each nest of naked mole rats has a single breeding queen. Worker rats dig tunnels, forage for food, and protect the queen's new litters.*

Reproduction

△ *The male bird of paradise attempts to attract a female by dancing and displaying his feathers. His would-be partner scrutinizes the dance. If she is impressed, she will mate.*

No plant or animal lives forever. Each organism alive today is descended from countless generations, all of which have reproduced successfully. The production of offspring is therefore one of the most important priorities of every animal and plant, and they all show great energy and ingenuity in making sure they succeed. Strategies for reproduction vary widely. Birds lay shelled eggs, mammals produce live young, and some insects even inject their eggs into the bodies of caterpillars. Yet the basics remain the same—an animal must ensure that sperm meets egg. Each organism has its own proven methods of making sure the family line continues, methods that have evolved over very long periods of time. As these examples show, the evolution of reproduction has taken nature in many different directions.

Courtship

Reproduction often involves mating. But choosing a mate is difficult. Courtship is a method of judging how good a mate a prospective partner might be. Mammals and birds often perform dramatic courtship rituals. For example, male birds of paradise attract their females by displaying fabulously colored feathers and by dancing. Females choose the best male on offer, perhaps by judging the energy of the dancer, or by measuring the luster of his feathers.

◁ *Male fiddler crabs have one huge claw. Females prefer a big claw—it signifies strength.*

▷ *Frogs lay large amounts of frog spawn, but most of the developing tadpoles are doomed. Fish and herons will scoop up some; others will starve. Despite this high death rate, enough young frogs will survive to perpetuate the family line.*

Safety in numbers

Successful reproduction is not simply a matter of laying eggs or giving birth. It is important that the offspring survive, are healthy, and are likely to reproduce, too. For the family line to continue into the future, ideally a pair of animals should produce at least two surviving, healthy young. Some animals ensure this by seeking safety in numbers. A cod spawns millions of eggs, but most will be unfertilized or eaten by predators. Yet, by producing so many eggs, there is a good chance that two, at least, will develop fully into adults.

△ *This male waterbug is an excellent father. A female has glued a clutch of eggs onto his back. He takes care of them, floating near the surface to make sure they have enough oxygen.*

Monogamy and polygamy

Although many animals adopt the intensive parental care strategy, the roles of the male and female parents often vary. Monogamous males mate with one female each breeding season. Polygamous males mate with several females. The evolution of this difference seems to depend on whether the male is willing to rear offspring. Male birds are good fathers and take their fair share of looking after the young. Most mammals are polygamous—after fertilization, the young grow inside the mother and are then suckled by her, but the father has no further role. Yet many carnivorous mammals are monogamous. Males hunt while females and young remain safe in their lair.

Intensive parental care

One way to ensure the survival of some young is to produce a lot of them. But another common strategy is to invest time and energy in the young offspring, feeding them and making sure they are safe. This is only possible if the young are few in number. By treating them well, they are much more likely to survive. Mammals are good parents, partly because the fertilized egg and the fetus are nourished in the safety of the womb. Yet parental care has also evolved in many other animal groups, from fish to insects and amphibians.

◁ *Sea horses carry live young, but it is the male who takes on this job. The female lays her eggs inside the male, who simply fertilizes them. The embryos develop, nourished by their own yolk sacs. Finally, when they are ready, the 0.5-inch (1-cm)-long babies emerge and take cover in the weeds on the seabed.*

◁ *Cuckoos arrange excellent parental care—but in somebody else's home. The female cuckoo lays an egg in the nest of another species, leaving the young cuckoo to be reared by a foster mother.*

Hunting and Feeding

▽ *A hunting bat's squeaks will bounce off a flying insect and be picked up by the bat's echo equipment. To avoid being located, moths have evolved soft, fluffy wings, which may absorb the bat's calls, rather than reflect them.*

For animals, feeding is a priority. Unlike plants, they cannot get nutrition just from the sun and the soil. They must work hard to find food—some must kill it—and assimilate it into their bodies. If an animal fails to eat, it becomes weak; it will be less likely to avoid being eaten itself, to find a mate, and to produce offspring. Although feeding is such a basic need, different species have evolved many different methods of finding food. How an animal feeds is as much an adaptation as its skeleton, its coloration, or its nervous system. Seeds, vegetation, plankton, fish, and small mammals are all excellent sources of nutrition. But to take advantage of them, hungry animals need the right teeth, the correct digestive system, and the appropriate behavior.

Feeding strategies

There are a few basic strategies for feeding. Herbivores rely on plants for nutrition. They grind up grass, nibble berries, and suck up nectar. Carnivores attack and kill other animals or search for carrion. Detritus-feeders, such as oysters and mussels, filter tiny particles of food from the surrounding water. In every case, an animal's body and behavior is well adapted for its chosen food. An oyster sits on the seabed, hardly moving. Its food comes to it. But a lion needs stealth, agility, and power to stalk and seize its prey.

◁ *Even the single-celled organism paramecium has a mouth, the ectoproct, filled with long hairs that waft in drifting bacteria. Like complex animals, a paramecium senses its food, and will set off purposefully to find a meal.*

Browsing and feasting

Animals vary in how often they need to feed. Birds are homeothermic—their body temperature is constantly warm, making their organs, and especially their brain, work quickly. But to keep warm, they must search for food constantly. Large herbivores, such as elephants, are also steady feeders. To get enough nutrition, they need to process a huge bulk of vegetation. Meat eating, however, is a riskier lifestyle. For tigers, not every hunt is successful, and they may eat only once every three days. Carnivores like this feed in a series of big feasts, followed by fasts. As for deep-sea fish, their specialty is waiting. Often they have to wait many days before a dead animal drifts down from above.

▷ *An anglerfish uses a light to lure its prey. A huge mouth ensures that when a rare meal appears, it does not escape.*

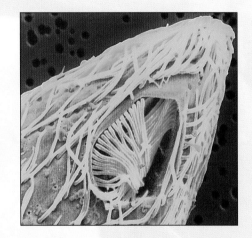

Feeding and the balance of nature

The act of feeding is crucial for the individual, but it can also help other organisms, and can be vital for promoting the well-being of the ecosystem. When bees search for nectar in flowers, they also carry away a cargo of pollen, which will fertilize other plants of the same species. In forests, millions of worms and insects feed on dead leaves and bark, recycling the plants' nutrients and eventually releasing them into the soil. One result of feeding is that populations of animals stay at stable levels—if herbivores increase in number, so do carnivores, and they help bring the herbivore population down again. Each animal's behavior is part of a wider picture—by feeding one another, animals and plants maintain the balance of nature.

▷ *Pollen rubs off on a bee's body as it feeds on the flower's sweet nectar. When the bee carries it to another flower, the pollen triggers the plant's reproduction.*

Senses for feeding

All animals use their senses to help them feed. Land animals often rely on their eyes and ears, and in the darkness of the sea a shark's sense of smell alerts it to a meal. In some cases, senses have become very specialized. Bats use "echolocation," where they emit high-pitched squeaks and listen for the echoes that bounce off their prey; a peregrine falcon can spot smaller birds flying up to 5 miles (8 km) away. Once again, evolution fine-tunes behavior, nervous systems, and body structure to give each animal the best chance of finding food.

Hunting in groups

Wolves and hunting dogs can kill prey ten times their own weight when they work as a group, so, in most cases, the animals cooperate to succeed. At the start of a hunt, the pack of dogs darts through a herd of prey, triggering a stampede. Quickly, the pack homes in on a weak individual, perhaps a straggling youngster. Working together, they corner it, leap on it from all sides, and bring it down. Even after the kill, cooperation continues—hunting dogs and wolves regurgitate food for their hungry young.

▷ *After a long chase, African wild dogs pull down an antelope. The dogs cooperate during the hunt, by taking turns to be the lead chaser, and by setting up an ambush. At the kill, the dogs work together to fend off the desperate kicks of the dying animal, while using their teeth to slash and tear the strong hide. Even when the prey is weak or small, the dogs risk being injured, so they cooperate to kill their food quickly.*

Aggression

Animals are purposeful. They need food, water, and often a mate. These objectives are vital for survival, so evolution favors behavior that helps the animal get what it wants. Usually an animal goes about its business peacefully. For example, the different species of birds in the woods largely ignore each other. They eat different food and use different materials for their nests. There is no reason to fight. But conflict is sometimes inevitable, and is most common between members of the same species. They eat the same food and like the same kind of territory. Getting a fair share of it is not always easy.

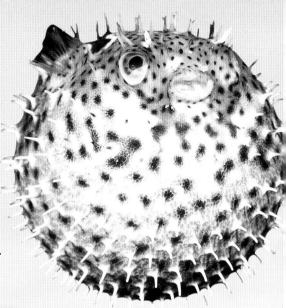

△ *The puffer makes an aggressive display by inflating like a ball and raising its spines. The startling effect often makes a fight unnecessary.*

△ *The South American arrow poison frog will wrestle an intruding rival to defend his territory.*

△ *Stags use their antlers in battle if necessary. However, real fights are rare. During the mating season, their roaring often establishes who is strongest.*

Territorial disputes

Animals often choose a patch of land and claim it as their own. They police its boundaries. Wild cats mark their territory with urine, and birds sing loudly to show that a tree is occupied. The territory may be a source of food, or a safe area for raising a family, and it is fiercely defended from members of the same species.

Aggressive displays

Aggression may get an animal what it needs, but fights can go wrong. Injuries can be fatal. Evolution has thus equipped animals not only with weapons, but with ways of avoiding a real fight. When stags are searching for females, the males stage mock fights and roar at each other. The intensity of the roar is a sign of strength. The weaker stags often know they are beaten just by listening

▷ *The frilled lizard warns rivals by suddenly opening the frill on his neck. This emphasizes— and exaggerates—his size and strength.*

Equipped for battle

If animals are going to fight, they have to be equipped. The size of a stag's antlers may warn off a rival, but if not, its antlers will be used for fighting. Giant horns have also evolved in insects, especially beetles. Stag beetles are 2 inches (5 cm) long, with strong armor and massive "antlers." The antlers are often used in battle, as rivals struggle to overturn each other.

△ Topis avoid a fight by completing a series of mock challenges. They assess each other's strength, and the weaker one backs off.

◁ Stag beetles' "antlers" are actually enormously enlarged mouthparts. Fights end when one beetle is left helpless on its back.

Undersea aggression

Aggression is not restricted to fast-moving animals. Sea anemones creep slowly over rocks, but if one is challenged by another, trouble flares. Anemones are soft-bodied and cannot attack using antlers or pincers. Instead, they have stinging tentacles, which push intruders out of their territory and fire a series of poisonous harpoons.

◁ Beadlet anemones have sophisticated weapon systems. The animal on the left is stinging the yellow intruder using harpoons clustered on its tentacles.

The last resort

In most cases, animals avoid fights. Their ritualized displays, such as roaring or antler waving, often produce a peaceful settlement. But when fighting does break out, the results can be serious. The most dramatic examples occur when males fight over mates. Breeding elephant seals can inflict real damage on each other. Males guarding two or three females will attack any other male that comes close.

▷ When bull elephant seals fight, blood flows. Heads lunge and teeth slash into blubber. These battles scar both animals for life.

△ *Monarch butterflies fill the Mexican forests, waiting for the spring. When warm days return, millions will set off on the return trip to Canada.*

Migration

Seasonal changes in temperature and other conditions often mean that a species' winter feeding ground is far from an area suitable for summer breeding. For this and other reasons, many animals migrate vast distances to survive. Their urge to travel has evolved—it is a result of natural selection, just as much as wing structure or coat color. The instinct is so strong that a hungry sea bird, migrating toward its feeding ground, will ignore food thrown out from the ships below. It struggles to reach the same site that countless generations of birds have visited, and only death can divert it from its course.

The butterflies' migration

One of the most amazing of all animal migrations is that of the monarch butterfly, which migrates each fall from Canada to Mexico to spend the winter there. In the spring, the swarms head north again, but on the way, many lay eggs and die. The hatchlings continue north to Canada, to feed and lay more eggs. The round trip is 3,750 miles (6,000 km)—an enormous distance for an insect with a wingspan of only 3.5 inches (9 cm).

The green turtles' journey

Green turtles hatch from eggs laid on remote beaches in Central and South America. The infant turtles crawl to the surf and disperse across the Atlantic Ocean. Months later, in an incredible feat of navigation, the turtles return to the very same beaches to lay their own eggs.

△ *Wildebeest show the determination of all migrating animals. No obstacle, not even a river's raging torrents, can halt their journey.*

The trek of the wildebeest

Each year, wildebeest travel more than 1,000 miles (1,600 km) across the African Serengeti Plains. Their trek is dictated by rainfall—or the lack of it. Young wildebeest are born during the rainy season when grass is plentiful. But every May and June, as the rains cease and the grass dies, the wildebeest migrate. Huge herds travel traditional routes, losing thousands to predators and starvation, until they reach their summer watering holes.

◁ *Green turtles may use the earth's magnetic field to help them navigate thousands of miles across the open ocean.*

The journey of the salmon

The Atlantic salmon is a migrant fish, but it travels only at the beginning and end of its life. Adult fish live in the ocean, but travel back up the river where they were born to breed. The salmon use the contours of the seabed and their sense of smell to navigate. Once they reach the estuary, the salmon stop feeding and use all their energy to swim upriver. As they approach the breeding grounds, the water becomes fast and the way steep. The fish have to jump and struggle to reach their goal. Finally, the adults lay their eggs and release their sperm, then quickly die. It is the young hatchlings who will swim back to the ocean, returning one day to the ancestral river.

△ *Salmon leap the rapids high up in a mountain river. These adults have not fed since they left the sea, hundreds of miles behind them. They will only rest when they reach the breeding ground.*

The voyage of the arctic tern

The champion migrant of all creatures is the arctic tern. Every year, its migratory round trip takes it from the Arctic to the Antarctic and back again—an annual flight of nearly 16,000 miles (25,000 km). Terns breed in the Arctic, laying eggs and feeding the chicks during the summer. When winter approaches, they set off to the other side of the world, where the antarctic seas are full of fish. After feeding for three months, they travel back to breed.

▽ *An arctic tern can live for more than 25 years. Since it migrates every year, it flies a staggering 400,000 miles (1 million km) during its lifetime.*

Terns from western Canada travel south down the Pacific coast.

Arctic breeding grounds
Terns stay here throughout the arctic summer (May–July).

Asia

Terns from Asia and Europe travel south down the coast of Africa.

Terns flying north fan out across the Atlantic Ocean.

North America

Pacific Ocean

South America

Atlantic Ocean

Antarctic feeding grounds
Terns remain here throughout the antarctic summer (November–February).

▷ *By traveling from one side of the world to the other, arctic terns are able to take advantage of both arctic and antarctic summers, when the sun never sets. By doing so, the birds enjoy more hours of daylight each year than any other living thing.*

Communication

Organisms developed communication because it helps survival. Smells in the air, for example, can warn an animal that it has entered another's territory, allowing it to retreat before a fight breaks out. This benefits both animals, so evolution favors both the ability to make a signal and the skill to understand it. Communication ranges from simple signals, where a color, chemical, or sound produces a change in another animal's behavior, to the complexity of human language, where sounds are used to exchange abstract ideas and even to mislead.

△ *Flowers use color to attract bees and other insects. The system evolved because the insects benefit, too, getting a good meal of nectar.*

▷ *Sound signals can travel great distances and are not blocked by obstacles such as trees. Studies have shown that each wolf howls with its own distinctive sound.*

Sound

Communication evolves according to circumstance. Sound is a good way of signaling when visibility is poor in woodland or jungle. Many songbirds live in the woods and can most effectively assert their territory by singing. Sometimes sound can be used for tricking others. Great tits have up to eight different songs—by singing them in quick succession, they can make other great tits think that the woods are already full. Sounds can be dangerous, too. When crickets chirp to attract a mate, they risk alerting hungry birds. Once he attracts a female, the male lowers his volume to reduce the risk of being eaten.

Visual signals

Visual signals work over a long distance and have the advantage of traveling quickly. Unlike chemical signals, which float on the wind, visual signals instantly identify the sender. This is useful when brightly colored plumage or a spectacular dance is used to attract a mate. Most visual signals cannot be used at night, and they do not travel around barriers. They are important, therefore, when visibility is good, as on the African plains. When herbivores run away from predators, they may demonstrate their speed and strength by jumping in the air and darting from side to side. This tells the predator that they are extremely agile and will be hard to catch.

▷ *This springbok is "stotting"—leaping up and down to signal its fitness to a marauding lioness to prevent her from trying to hunt it.*

Chemical signals

Insects often use scent to communicate with each other. Females release mating pheromones, chemicals that drift downwind and are recognized by members of the same species. Even one or two molecules can have a powerful effect, luring males in search of the female. But there are disadvantages. Strong winds can blow all the pheromones away too quickly; on a still night, the scent will just accumulate around the female. Not much information can be sent in this way, apart from the basic signal "female upwind." Scents cannot be directed easily, nor altered quickly enough to form complex messages in the way that sounds or visual signals can.

△ *Fireflies are unusual because they use a visual signal at night. Their flashing abdomens are filled with a photochemical mix and release controlled sequences of light flashes to attract a mate.*

△ *Humans often use artificial means to intensify a visual message. This man is wearing war paint.*

Multichannel communication

Animals may use more than one method of signaling to get their message across. Ants that come across a dying caterpillar will rush back to their colony, leaving a trail of scent. Once in the nest, they perform an agitated dance for their companions, who then run outside and pick up the chemical trail. But the most versatile communicators are probably humans, who back up language with many types of facial gestures, body language, and dress.

Sophisticated expressions

Humans are very proud of their communication skills. They use language to express their emotions and to discuss complex ideas, such as evolution. Furthermore, the ability to talk is backed up by the skills of reading and writing, which allow spoken ideas to be made permanent and faithfully communicated years later. But humans are still sensitive to more basic signals, and may be strongly affected by chemical and visual signals from other people without fully realizing it.

▷ *Chimpanzees have a rich variety of facial expressions and can clearly communicate sadness and happiness to each other.*

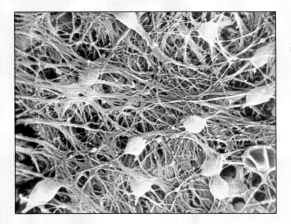

On Being Human

The story of human evolution began four million years ago, with a group of apes in the African jungle. It has led to *Homo sapiens*, the talking primate that dominates the world. To discover how this happened, scientists examine fossils and stone tools, and use DNA testing to compare the fossils with living humans and wild apes. So far, the story remains incomplete. Although scientists disagree on the details, there is no mystery about why humans thrive. They combine intelligence and complex social organization to produce a level of creativity unique in the animal world.

△ *Billions of interconnected neurons fill the human brain. Its size and complexity is at the root of our species' success. Social bonding is crucial, too—long years of childcare ensure that huge amounts of vital information are passed from parent to offspring.*

The bipedal breakthrough

It is no accident that the world's most intelligent animals evolved from apes. These clever, social animals already organized themselves in groups. But four million years ago, a group of apes evolved that were able to stand on their hind legs. As their hands were freed from walking and climbing, they could become more agile. Ape fingers, which were already good at holding and twisting, could become ideal for making tools, provided they were guided by a strong brain.

The importance of brainpower

After bipedalism, the second important step was the evolution of the brain. Over the last four million years, the brain has become bigger and bigger. The first bipedal apes had a brain half the size of *Homo habilis*, an early human. Modern humans, *Homo sapiens*, have a brain more than twice that size. The increases were gradual, but steady. At every stage, an agile hand and an intelligent brain could work well together. They depended on each other and encouraged each to develop constantly.

◁ *Manual agility and exceptional toolmaking ability are at the heart of human evolution and its extraordinary success.*

△ *For many thousands of years, humans have dominated and domesticated other animals for a variety of purposes. Human intelligence allows us to adapt other species to suit ourselves.*

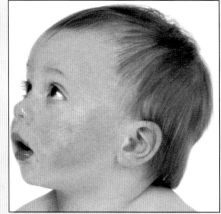

◁ *The story of human evolution is captured by these photographs of a young chimpanzee and a baby. Both spend periods learning from their parents and through play. However, each new generation of chimpanzees grows up in much the same environment as the last, requiring no new skills. But human evolution has created a restless species that is able to change its environment continually. Each new generation has to adapt to these changes, and this baby will spend much of her life absorbing new skills.*

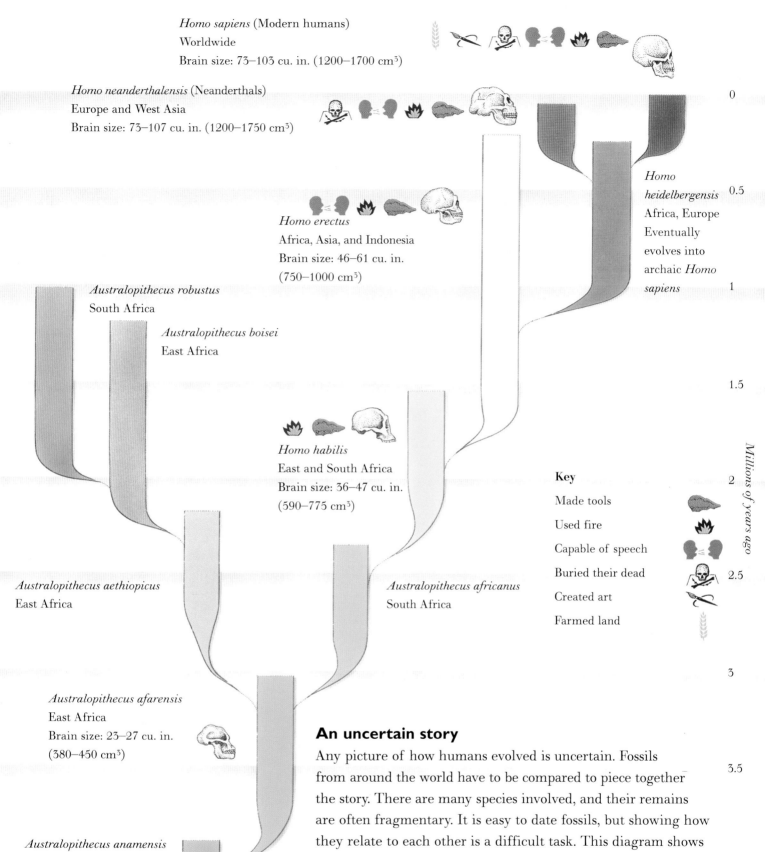

Homo sapiens (Modern humans)
Worldwide
Brain size: 73–103 cu. in. (1200–1700 cm³)

Homo neanderthalensis (Neanderthals)
Europe and West Asia
Brain size: 73–107 cu. in. (1200–1750 cm³)

Homo heidelbergensis
Africa, Europe
Eventually evolves into archaic *Homo sapiens*

Homo erectus
Africa, Asia, and Indonesia
Brain size: 46–61 cu. in. (750–1000 cm³)

Australopithecus robustus
South Africa

Australopithecus boisei
East Africa

Homo habilis
East and South Africa
Brain size: 36–47 cu. in. (590–775 cm³)

Australopithecus aethiopicus
East Africa

Australopithecus africanus
South Africa

Key

Made tools

Used fire

Capable of speech

Buried their dead

Created art

Farmed land

Australopithecus afarensis
East Africa
Brain size: 23–27 cu. in. (380–450 cm³)

Australopithecus anamensis
East Africa

Ardipithecus ramidus
East Africa

Millions of years ago

0
0.5
1
1.5
2
2.5
3
3.5
4
4.5
5

An uncertain story

Any picture of how humans evolved is uncertain. Fossils from around the world have to be compared to piece together the story. There are many species involved, and their remains are often fragmentary. It is easy to date fossils, but showing how they relate to each other is a difficult task. This diagram shows one possible picture of the human family tree. It shows a series of connections, suggesting how one species gave rise to another before dying out. The connections are controversial. There are no fossils that show the species actually transforming. These times of change were quick, so there was less chance of the "missing links" becoming fossilized. Yet the overall pattern is clear, showing the australopithecine apes evolving into early humans, and then into modern humans.

▽ Australopithecus afarensis *lived in groups, in or near forests. They were good climbers, able to scale trees for fruit—and sometimes meat— but their ability to walk upright on their hind legs allowed them to explore the new, open environments of the East African plains.*

◁ *Olduvai Gorge in Tanzania is one of the most important sites for scientists studying human ancestry. It is part of the Great Rift Valley, a giant fault system running through eastern Africa. Australopithecine remains have been found here, along with the bones of later humans.*

THE EVOLUTION OF HUMANS

Upright Apes

Like every other organism on the planet, humans have distant ancestors and a long history. Our own species, *Homo sapiens*, evolved only 130,000 years ago, but the primate branch that leads to us stretches back much farther. The fossils are very rare, and the full picture is uncertain, yet progress is being made. New fossils have been found, and there are more accurate ways of determining their age. The evidence shows that human evolution began four million years ago in East Africa, with a group of animals called the australopithecines.

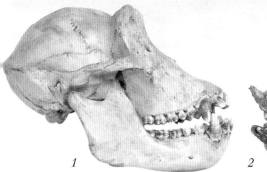

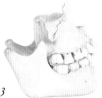

◁ *The jaws of (1) a chimpanzee, (2) an australopithecine, and (3) a modern human. Although 2 is apelike, it has small canines, like 3. This implies australopithecines are the ancestors of humans.*

Australopithecines appear

Today East Africa has vast, dry plains with few trees. But millions of years ago, it was covered with thick jungle and was home to many apes. The apes were fine climbers, able to swing out of danger. Four million years ago, the land began to dry out. The jungle thinned into woods and grassland. It was then that a new group of apes appeared. They could stand up and move quickly across the plains. These were the australopithecines.

A key advantage

Australopithecine brains were not much bigger than those of apes. Yet their upright walk allowed them to move faster and to spot danger from farther away. As the land grew more open, the habitats of ordinary apes vanished. But australopithecines survived, probably living in groups and cooperating in hunts. Eventually, some developed larger brains, a more athletic build, and the ability to make tools. These would be the first true humans.

Between apes and humans

Many types of *Australopithecus* have been found, but the most research has been done on *Australopithecus afarensis*, which lived around 3.5 million years ago. Its skull is apelike, but its foot, toe, and thigh bones are all similar to those of humans. From this, it is clear that the animal could walk upright. The teeth were rounded, with grinding surfaces, so *Australopithecus* was probably largely vegetarian. Like modern apes, there was a big difference in size between the sexes—males averaged just over 4 feet (120 cm) and females 3.5 feet (100 cm) tall. This was still an ape, but one with many human features.

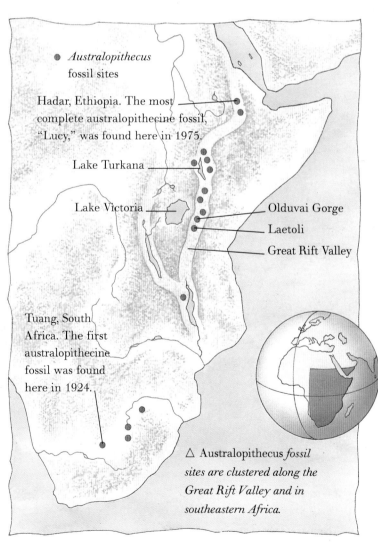

● *Australopithecus* fossil sites

Hadar, Ethiopia. The most complete australopithecine fossil, "Lucy," was found here in 1975.

Lake Turkana

Lake Victoria

Olduvai Gorge
Laetoli
Great Rift Valley

Tuang, South Africa. The first australopithecine fossil was found here in 1924.

△ Australopithecus *fossil sites are clustered along the Great Rift Valley and in southeastern Africa.*

The First Humans

The evolution of hominids—humans and their bipedal ancestors—is barely understood. Fossil remains are rare and usually so fragmentary that guesswork is needed to piece together the clues. However, in 1984, the discovery in Kenya of an almost complete skeleton made one part of the story much clearer. The child, known as "Turkana boy," had died 1.5 million years ago, but displayed many recognizable human features, including a large brain and a fully upright posture. He is the best fossil evidence for a key link in our evolutionary story, a species now named *Homo erectus*. Along with *Homo habilis*—their predecessors—these were the first true humans, capable of making a great variety of tools. *Homo erectus* was a hugely successful species. It survived for more than a million years, with its population extending across Africa and Asia.

△ Homo habilis *lived 2 million years ago. Their average brain size is 41 cu. in. (670 cm³)— this is 12 cu. in. (200 cm³) less than* Homo erectus *and half that of modern humans. Flaked rocks show they used simple tools.*

▷ Homo erectus *seems to have made many significant advances on previous hominids. It was the first species to use fire, and the first to create base camps around which the family group could live, learn, and play.*

Designs for life

To be human is to be a skilled toolmaker. By the time of "Turkana boy," humans were shaping stones into many varieties of scrapers and axes to help cut and chop food. The techniques used would have been passed down from parents to children. There is also evidence that *Homo erectus* used fire to keep warm and cook food—the first hominids known to do so. Evidence like this suggest that these early humans lived together and planned hunting expeditions. To do all these things requires a high level of intelligence.

△ *These tools—a scraper, a chopper, and a hand ax—were each carefully shaped by hammering flakes off a rock. Archaeologists learn about* Homo erectus's *way of life by studying the tools found at fossil sites. Early humans may have carried stones like this as a tool kit.*

Verbal communication

Early humans made a great step forward when they first developed tools and fire. To use them properly—to organize successful hunts or to protect the home—they had to be able to talk to each other. *Homo erectus* had a voice box able to make a great variety of sounds, and a large brain capable of interpreting their meaning.

Work and play

Homo erectus would have lived in camps close to water and food supplies. While some of the group departed on a hunt, other adults would remain behind with the children. There were many jobs to do—the fire had to be kept lit and tools prepared for the next hunt. Like modern *Homo sapiens*, the children would have used their long childhood to watch adults and learn survival skills. They were relatively safe in the camps and could play without fear, pretending to hunt and learning to carve tools.

The Rise of Homo sapiens

Our species, *Homo sapiens*, stands out from earlier humans because of the size of its brain and the sophistication of its behavior. Like their ancestors, early *Homo sapiens* lived in groups, usually in caves. But these caves were not just for shelter. Sometimes, far down in the darkness, the walls were painted with pictures of animals and hunts. Scientists have also found graves of *Homo sapiens* in the caves, with the bones carefully arranged. These new humans marked a death with a burial, and even a ceremony. They were sophisticated in other ways, too. They learned to make tools from bones and antlers as well as from stone, and carved them with a craftsman's eye.

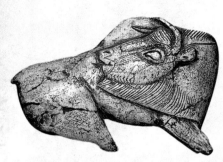

△ *About 40,000 years ago, people began carving bone. This buffalo is carved from reindeer antler.*

Worldwide success

The earliest fossils of *Homo sapiens*, found in Africa, are 130,000 years old. But fossils elsewhere are much younger—in Europe they are only 40,000 years old. This is explained by the "Out of Africa" theory, which says that modern humans evolved only in East Africa, and migrated worldwide from there.

△ *This French cave painting shows a horse painted on a horse-shaped rock and an outline of a hand. Paintings like this are often in inaccessible places, and may have religious significance.*

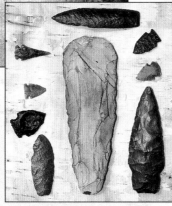

△ *Human tools became lighter and more varied. These arrowheads are 7,000 years old and have been shaped with great skill.*

◁ *When* Homo sapiens *appeared, so did storytelling. By talking about his past, this old man gives his listeners useful advice. Skills like this ensure that human culture keeps adapting.*

A new level of intelligence

For two million years, early human brains had been growing larger, and intelligence had steadily increased. *Homo erectus* had discovered fire, was an experienced user of tools, and may have used a simple form of language. With the evolution of *Homo sapiens*, human intelligence reached a completely different level. People could then discuss abstract ideas, such as the future and the past. They could use language to comfort each other or to give advice. They made ornaments by drilling holes in bones or shells to make necklaces. They made cave paintings of animals, human figures, and patterns, creating many beautiful works of art, which often seem full of spiritual meaning.

The path to modern humans

When *Homo sapiens* first evolved in Africa, their tools were simple and their language primitive. Yet these humans were alert and active, interested in exploring new environments. As they moved into Asia and Europe, they had to rely on each other for survival. Learning fast was important. Information about the landscape and about the dangerous —or useful—animals it contained was quickly shared. These continual challenges, and their solutions, gradually gave rise to human culture. By 40,000 years ago, the people living in Africa, Europe, and Asia were similar to us. They honored their dead, made many sophisticated tools, and spoke complex languages.

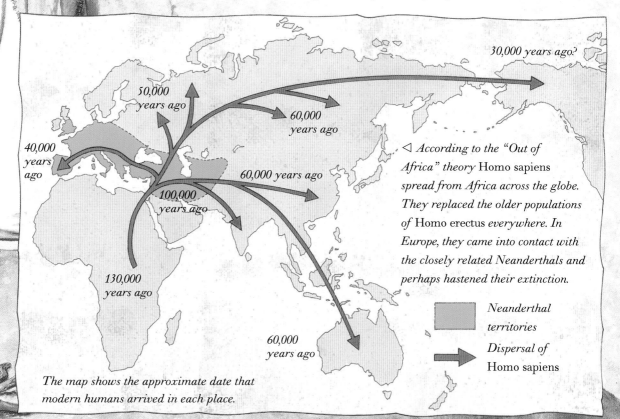

30,000 years ago?

50,000 years ago

60,000 years ago

40,000 years ago

60,000 years ago

100,000 years ago

130,000 years ago

60,000 years ago

60,000 years ago

◁ *According to the "Out of Africa" theory* Homo sapiens *spread from Africa across the globe. They replaced the older populations of* Homo erectus *everywhere. In Europe, they came into contact with the closely related Neanderthals and perhaps hastened their extinction.*

Neanderthal territories

Dispersal of Homo sapiens

The map shows the approximate date that modern humans arrived in each place.

▷ *This shelter was built out of mammoth tusks by modern* Homo sapiens *30,000 years ago. Their creative and adaptive ability may have ensured their survival, while their close relatives, the Neanderthals, died out.*

▽ *Neanderthals and* Homo sapiens *both spoke, but probably did not understand each other. Fossils cannot reveal whether their meetings were friendly or ended up in fighting. Perhaps* Homo sapiens *spoke faster, thought faster, and were more aggressive than Neanderthals.*

△ *Modern humans may have begun to domesticate wolves 100,000 years ago for use in hunting.*

THE EVOLUTION OF HUMANS

The Neanderthal Mystery

When *Homo sapiens* arrived in Europe 40,000 years ago, they found it inhabited by Neanderthals. These heavily-built people were well adapted to Ice Age Europe, and had evolved there long before. It is unclear how Neanderthals are related to *Homo sapiens*—they may have had the same recent ancestor—but they were similar in many ways. Both used fire, made tools, buried their dead, and were good communicators. However, soon after *Homo sapiens*'s arrival, the Neanderthals disappeared. Despite being less adapted to the cold, *Homo sapiens* flourished, and the Neanderthals died out. No one knows why. *Homo sapiens* may have been better at building shelters and finding food. Gradually, the Neanderthals retreated until they died out on the shores of Portugal. From that point 30,000 years ago, only one type of human has remained—*Homo sapiens*.

△ *The Neanderthals buried their dead, sometimes scattering them with flowers. This implies very strong social bonds.*

Adapted to the cold

At the time of the Neanderthals, an ice age had swept over Europe. Many aspects of their anatomy suggest they were adapted to harsh conditions. Their arms and legs were short, reducing surface area to conserve heat. The strong muscle attachments on the bones show that Neanderthals were very muscular and used to heavy work. They had jutting faces and noses, perhaps allowing air to be warmed more thoroughly before it entered the lungs.

Neanderthals and modern humans

Neanderthals evolved in Europe and seemed perfectly adapted to the problems of living in an ice age. Fossil evidence shows that they butchered their meat efficiently and had teeth strong enough to crush bone and tear hide. Neanderthals had a home life, too, and a language. Yet there are no clues to their extinction. There is no cave art describing fights between humans and Neanderthals— or cooperation. If there was conflict, there is no record.

What happened when they met?

The two kinds of humans must have met from time to time. Scientists can only guess at what happened. Perhaps Neanderthals were afraid of the newcomers—people who could run quicker than they could and make better tools. It is likely that the groups behaved very differently, and that lack of understanding led to distrust. However, there have been theories that interbreeding took place, and that Neanderthal genes live on today in modern human beings.

△ *Neanderthals were skilled makers of tools. More than 60 different stone implements have been found.*

Why Humans Are Successful

△ *This monastery in Jericho rises from the arid desert landscape. Around the world, humans have been able to transform most environments.*

Over billions of years of evolution, many millions of species have arisen and become extinct. Whether bird, insect, or mammal, every species is, in its own way, successful. For a time at least, each is superbly adapted. Its members can reproduce, and their genes are passed from one generation to another. Sometimes this success continues for long periods of time— bacteria evolved 3.5 billion years ago, and are still here today. But *Homo sapiens*—modern humans—who evolved only 130,000 years ago, seem different from all other living organisms. Only humans have language. Only humans can study art and science, and write about the past. And only humans can learn so much that their behavior can be different from their parents'.

The agricultural revolution

For thousands of years, humans lived by hunting animals and gathering wild plants. They moved in small groups, following the migration of large herds. The world's population stayed steady, with about 10 million people—the same as the population of a large, modern city. Then 12,000 years ago, probably in the Middle East, there was a change. People discovered grasses that they could plant themselves, such as corn and wheat. It was no longer necessary to keep moving. Now people could settle where the soil was good, to work the land and plant seeds.

New communities

Agriculture encouraged the growth of larger communities. Though hunting continued, the home was now a source of food as well, with regular crops for harvesting each year. Around 10,000 years ago, goats and sheep were domesticated and kept in herds. Humans could now eat meat, even if there were no wild animals for miles around. Slowly, from this time on, the human population began to grow.

△ *Agriculture meant that less time needed to be spent finding food, which allowed complex societies to develop. Egyptian civilization was based on the fertile lands of the Nile River.*

◁ *Contemporary Chinese rice cultivation shows how agriculture still depends on intensive work and an ability to shape the land. In many places, terraces and irrigation are both essential for rice to grow.*

△ *Tokyo at night is filled with neon signs. Cities are not just places to live, but zones where entertainment, work, and recreation are mixed closely together. The development of cities depends on technology and on the ability of humans to specialize as farmers, traders, builders, and teachers, each contributing to society in a small way.*

The vital role of learning

Education is vital for humans. Because individuals can both teach and learn, skills can be taught to children. Schools pass on skills and also teach children the rules of their society. However, most learning takes place outside school, at home or with friends, and this is less controlled. Movies, music, fashion, books, and architecture change and influence people all the time. Human society evolves continually, but more in its culture than its biology.

Technology

Even when they first evolved, humans stood out from other animals because of their tools. By 40,000 years ago, humans were making sophisticated axes and knives from stones. Copper began to be used 8,000 years ago, and bronze 2,000 years ago. In the last few hundred years, strong metals, such as steel, have revolutionized technology. Endless industrial innovations have led to engines, mass production, and most recently, the computer revolution.

> *Humans are beginning to develop computers that mimic their own shape and intelligence. "Cog" is an android robot that can use its vision, hearing, and touch to find things, pick them up, and then evaluate them.*

Mastering the environment

By 1999, the world's population had reached 6 billion. Most people now live in cities, and it is in cities that the extent of human success can be seen most clearly. Humans build their environment to fulfill their needs. With roads, heating, and telecommunications, it is human surroundings that change, not the humans themselves. This has never happened before in evolution. Humans protect themselves from natural selection by removing many environmental threats. But this strategy may not work. Today's population creates a lot of pollution, and when people crowd together in huge numbers, contagious diseases are a real risk.

◁ *Formal education is unique to humans. Skills learned by one generation are not lost because they can be easily passed to the next. The rapid changes seen in cultural evolution depend partly on highly efficient education systems.*

Genomes and Gene Therapy

When *Homo sapiens* evolved, the potential to manipulate evolution arose, too. For thousands of years, people bred animals and plants, artificially selecting the variations, despite knowing nothing about genes. Dairy cattle were bred to produce high volumes of milk, while plants were selected to give high yields. By breeding the best specimens, useful genes from different individuals were combined. But with today's knowledge of genetics, scientists can select genes from one species and insert them into a completely different species. For example, a useful gene from a fish can be inserted into a tomato. Artificial genetic manipulation gives people the power to change themselves, as well as other organisms.

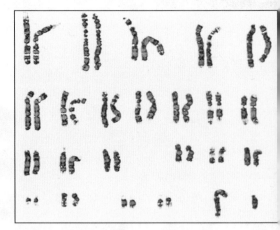

△ The 23 pairs of chromosomes in a human cell contain at least 80,000 genes. The Human Genome Project will have identified each one by 2003.

The Human Genome Project

New genetic skills rely on knowing what individual genes do and where they are. The Human Genome Project, a series of experiments being carried out in laboratories across the world, seeks to unravel the mystery of genes. The "genome" is the number of genes in a full set of chromosomes, and the Genome Project aims to identify each one, and work out the sequences of the three billion chemical bases in their DNA code.

▽ Gene research may profoundly affect our approach to the human body. Babies may be cured of inherited diseases long before they are born.

Gene therapy

Good health depends on your genes working correctly. The disease cystic fibrosis is caused by a faulty gene. This affects the cells in the lungs, causing a buildup of mucus. Breathing becomes difficult, so physical therapy and other treatments help clear the lungs. Scientists have now found the faulty gene. If normal genes replace the abnormal ones, the lungs may start working correctly and cure the disease. But for this "gene therapy" to work, scientists must first find a safe method of transporting new genes into the cell nucleus.

◁ Medical researchers around the world are expanding our knowledge of genes at breakneck speed. It is now known that cancer and heart disease are partly genetic in origin. The race is on to find the cures.

Germ-line therapy

When genes become faulty, the problem is likely to be passed to any offspring. So inherited diseases often remain in the family, even if one person is cured. In germ-line therapy, it is the sperm or egg that has genes replaced. These alterations will be permanent—the next generation will pass on the changes. Yet, if the therapy goes wrong, causing a new disease, this might permanently affect a family. For this reason, germ-line therapy is not allowed.

Designer babies

Altering genes may not only be used to prevent diseases. The power to manipulate the human genome could be used for other purposes. Height, eye color, and hair color are all controlled by genes. At the moment, no one knows how to manipulate them, but there is already a fear that parents of the future may wish to pay for changes to their babies' genes, in order to to control the way they look.

Genetically modified plants

Research into modifying plants genetically is controversial. Some people do not like eating food with altered genes. Scientists argue that the crops have already had their genes changed through centuries of breeding. Some modification helps crops resist diseases, or increases the harvest. Such technology may help some places avoid famine. Critics argue that these results can be achieved by better irrigation and government intervention.

Genetics and evolution

Governments are already making laws to regulate the new gene technologies, but it will be years before the full implications are known of this science. Genetics does have enormous potential for changing human society, for better or worse. In time, gene technologies could even affect evolution, by spreading particular genes across a whole population. The future of the human genome could be changed forever.

◁ *These baby mice have had a jellyfish gene inserted in them that makes them glow. The gene could help mark cancer cells as the cancer cells spread through the body.*

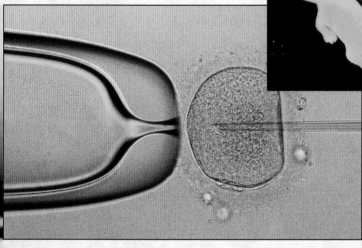

△ In vitro *fertilization is a modern fertility treatment. A female egg is extracted, then injected with sperm by a micropipette, as shown here. The fertilized egg is placed back inside the mother to grow. Such techniques could become part of germ-line therapy, altering the baby's genes forever.*

▷ *In the future, patients may be able to inhale new genes, inject them, or even rub them on as an ointment. This type of gene therapy would help cure serious diseases by introducing healthy genes into the body to replace faulty ones. Before this is possible, scientists have to figure out how to get the genes into the precise area of the body where they are needed.*

Cloning

△ Currently, skin cells are grown to make a continuous sheet that is used to help people with burns. These skin grafts are usually successful, but if the skin could be cloned from the patient, rejection of the new tissue would be less of a risk.

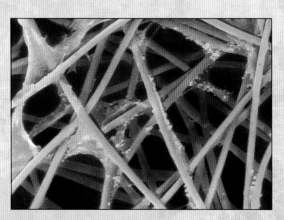

△ This human cartilage has been grown from the cells of a patient requiring treatment. The cartilage grows along artificial fibers that will disintegrate later. Because the cells have the patient's genes, the graft is genetically identical to the original.

A clone is an identical copy of a living thing. When two organisms are clones, each one has exactly the same set of genes. It can happen naturally, as when identical twins form from a single fertilized egg. Gardeners can make clones when they remove part of a stem from a plant and grow a new plant from it. All the cells in the stem have the same genes, so the new plant is identical. However, this does not normally happen with animals. Usually, their cells grow only as long as they are part of the organism. But scientists can now take animal cells and grow them separately—and the ramifications are immense.

Animal cloning

At first, scientists could only clone cells taken from very young animals, such as tadpoles. Then, in 1997, they managed to grow a lamb using a cell taken from an adult sheep's udder. The path was now clear to create complex animals without any of the genetic variation that underpins all normal life and evolution. The idea is appealing because scientists can control the genes contained in the cloned animal. If a sheep produces excellent milk, then lambs cloned from its cells will produce exactly the same milk. And if the adult sheep has been genetically modified, then all the modifications will turn up in the lambs, too.

Medical uses of animal cloning

Some sheep have already been genetically modified to produce medicine in their milk. Each time the adult is milked, the medicine is collected. By cloning cells from adults this way, scientists can over time create a flock of sheep, each identical, and each capable of producing the medicine. Meanwhile, genetically modified pigs are being developed to provide hearts for transplanting into humans. The pig's genes are altered so that the heart loses the proteins that indicate it comes from a pig. That way the heart is less likely to be rejected by its human recipient.

◁ Today, heart transplant surgery is possible only when another human heart becomes available. One day, modified pigs' hearts may be an alternative.

Human cloning

Some people think that cloning humans is a dangerous idea and should be prevented. In most countries, cloning humans is already illegal. In any case, cloning humans would not create identical people. Cloned babies must first grow up, and they will develop differently because no two people experience exactly the same life. But scientists hope they will be allowed to clone human organs grown in laboratories. If a patient will die without a new heart, their chances of survival are best if the transplanted heart is genetically similar. If a heart could be grown from their own cells, it would probably work very well.

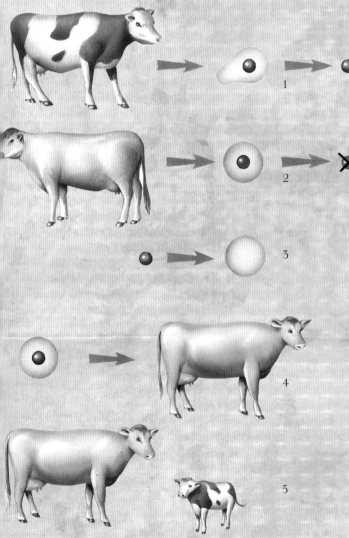

△ In the future, labs may be able to grow and store a range of human organs. Society must decide whether such facilities should be only for the seriously ill, or also for those with minor problems.

Conservation cloning

Some scientists have said that animals at risk of extinction should be cloned. Hundreds of pandas could be cloned from a single adult. Although this sounds like a good solution, it may not be. If there is no habitat for the pandas, the clones will not survive any better than the originals. Even if they do survive, the fact that they are genetically identical might harm the population. In the wild, genetic variation is important. A population of clones, being identical, could all be destroyed by a single germ.

▽ These cloned pigs were born on March 5, 2000. They were named Millie, Christa, Alexis, Carrel, and Dotcom.

△ In this cloning experiment, a cell is taken from a cow's udder, and its nucleus, containing its genetic information, is removed (1). An egg is taken from another cow, and its nucleus is destroyed (2). The nucleus from the udder is then placed inside the egg (3). The egg can then be stimulated to develop without fertilization, and is placed inside the womb of a surrogate mother (4). Some months later, if all goes well, calf clones of the original cow are born (5).

People and the World

Evolutionary history is a story of species emerging, flourishing, and then dying out. Humans are very successful animals, but our continued existence is not secure. War may ruin civilizations, and intense pollution or global warming could make large areas of the earth uninhabitable. With the population now over 6 billion people, scientists are asking whether the world can sustain everyone. But, unlike other animals, humans can engineer their own success. If we need more food, we can change the way we grow it to ensure higher yields. We can build houses to keep us comfortable in hostile terrain. Human ingenuity has the power to neutralize many environmental changes that challenge other species.

△ *Non-polluting energy may be vital in the future. Solar-powered cars can recharge in garages equipped with solar panels like this.*

▽ *Poverty and pollution are major problems in our overcrowded cities. Many people rely on the leftovers of the rich to survive. This South American garbage dump is being trawled for useful leftovers.*

Our destructive species

There are many aspects of human behavior that suggest that *Homo sapiens* will one day become extinct. Technology can be a dangerous force. In the 1900s, ingenious new weapons, from machine guns to nuclear bombs, killed millions of people—far more than ever before. Equally devastating has been the harm done to the natural world. Tropical rain forests have been bulldozed, and countless plants and animals have become extinct. By destroying irreplaceable natural riches, our species threatens the environments that we depend on for food and fuel—basically, our survival.

◁▽ *Poverty is a factor that leads to environmental destruction. Rain forests are burned down to make room for people needing land. Rhinoceroses are shot because one tusk can provide a year's wages for the poacher.*

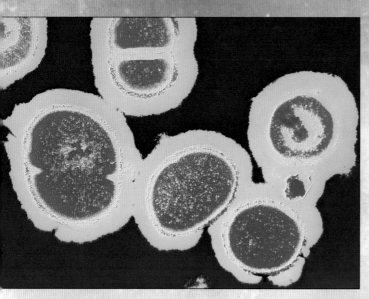

△ *The MRSA microbe is a "superbug," resistant to attack by any antibiotic. Microorganisms like this can change their form faster than scientists can invent new drugs to kill them.*

Our creative species

Despite our destructive power, humans also have a unique creative energy. Our ability to think means we can correct much of the damage we do to the world—and to ourselves. If an animal is on the verge of becoming extinct, we can freeze a sample of its cells, ready to clone new adults when the techniques are perfected. We can create protected environments to study how valuable ecosystems work. Most important, we can develop regulations and laws that can be enforced. Through the careful use of laws, wildlife, as well as people, can be protected.

▽▷ *Science attempts to control nature for the better. Giant pandas are artificially inseminated to save their species, while the* Biosphere II *project attempted to create a sealed ecosystem.*

The role of chance

Because people are both destructive and creative, it is hard to predict what problems humanity will face in the future. Only one thing is certain—chance will be an important factor. When people object to new technological inventions, such as genetically modified crops, it is the uncertainty they worry about. Because scientists do not fully understand how nature works, there is no evidence that crop alterations will not have dangerous side effects, or that humans will not encounter an outside threat, such as microbes that resist the strongest antibiotics. If we are to survive, we must continue to adapt to the ever-changing demands of environments that we have created.

▽ *At their best, the world's cities are not just cultural and commercial centers. They provide good places for people to live in harmony with open spaces, water, and vegetation.*

If Humans Die Out

It is hard enough to piece together evolution's past, but it is even more difficult to know what its future holds. Countless influences are at work during the evolution of any species, so scientists are not able to predict how even a single organism will evolve, let alone visualize the world in hundreds of millions of years. Currently, humans dominate the earth. But every species eventually either evolves or becomes extinct, and human beings are no exception. If we die out, we will leave many environments behind to be exploited by future species. As the ages pass, these species will become increasingly different from today's, although familiar body structures will continue to be used by these future organisms.

▽ *This future bird has evolved strengthening girders to supplement its skeleton. The girders resemble insect limbs, but are actually the greatly enlarged spines of feathers.*

▽ *This ferocious carnivore evolved from hooved herbivores. Evolution lengthened its incisors, turning them into the equivalent of sharp canines. The animal's digestive system adjusted to deal with the extra protein from meat.*

The extinction of humans

Humans have driven many species to extinction, both in the distant past and in recent years. The great mammals that lived 10,000 years ago, such as the giant ground sloth, were probably among the first to be hunted to extinction. Since then, the rate of extinction has accelerated as humans destroy more animal habitats. Yet if people themselves were to disappear, many of the large animals that are rare today—such as tigers, elephants, and wolves—would soon increase in number. They would encounter each other more often, and compete to exploit the newly empty habitats. Over a few million years, the gaps in the world's ecosytems would be filled by a host of new life forms.

▽ *Evolution is hard to predict. To evade predators, today's flying fish can propel itself out of the water using its powerful tail. Its large fins help it glide for short distances. Perhaps in the future it will evolve true wings and the ability to breathe air. It is impossible to say.*

△ *When humans disappear, their monuments will become overgrown. If they become extinct, all signs of their influence will quickly vanish, while evolution will ensure that their dominant position on Earth is filled by a variety of other species.*

Future oceans

Today's oceans have been seriously affected by human activities. Oil pollution regularly harms birds and coastal animals, while intensive fishing has reduced the stock of cod, herring, and salmon. Many whales have been hunted close to extinction. If humans die out, these populations might recover, and new predators might evolve to take advantage of the new glut of marine prey. Over millions of years, some drastic changes are likely. Perhaps some day birds will follow the example of mammals such as whales and dolphins, and adapt fully to life in the sea.

New landscapes

Future evolution will be affected constantly by the movement of tectonic plates. In 200 million years, for example, the American land mass might collide with Asia, creating a giant supercontinent. Huge new mountains will rise, and vast deserts will form in the center of the continent, driving many animals to extinction and forcing others to adapt to extreme habitats of cold and heat. Such changes have happened before, and will continue for as long as the earth survives.

△ *This remarkable aquatic bird has lost its body feathers, retaining them only on the wings. It now has a thick layer of blubber for insulation. It has also grown a strong, extended tail for steering under water.*

▽ *A small species of mammal has evolved into a long, legless desert animal that burrows in the sand. Unlike the reptilian snake of earlier eras, this creature undulates vertically, flexing its extended vertebrae.*

Future Humans

Homo sapiens first evolved in Africa 130,000 years ago, and then migrated across the entire globe. Fossils show that people's bodies changed somewhat during that time, becoming lighter and longer-limbed. But now, for humans, evolution appears to have stopped. Athough humans still vary genetically, it is rare for that variation to affect an individual's survival. If a habitat is hostile, buildings and machines are used to change it. It is also hard to imagine a group of people becoming so isolated that they develop their own unique genetic mix. In fact, the opposite is likely to happen—ease of travel will even out any remaining genetic differences between groups of people. But in the far future, the story may be different.

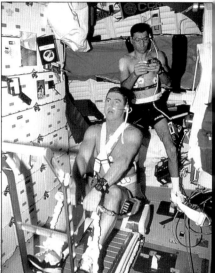

Future migrations

Evolution could produce new human species if some groups of people became isolated from the main population. In our world such isolation seems impossible. But in the distant future, there may be people traveling far into space. With the right technology, adventurers might start a new life on another planet, or even in other galaxies. Yet these pioneers, and their descendants, would be very likely to keep in touch with Earth. If they could travel so far away, they could probably travel back. Unless the isolation was complete, the genes would keep mixing, and a new species could not be formed.

△ The devastation one nuclear explosion caused at Hiroshima, Japan, in 1945 demonstrates the potential humans have for destruction. A major conflict could wipe out huge areas of the globe, leaving tiny pockets of humanity isolated from one another.

▽ Modern humans have always been too mobile for any group to become isolated. Race is nonexistent in evolutionary terms—it is just a gradual series of minor variations in response to geographic location.

Future catastrophe

Human evolution is only likely to restart if people lose control of the environment. Today, pollution is warming up the globe, and many habitats are being destroyed. Everyone hopes that the planet will remain inhabitable until this destruction is brought under control. But far in the future, the planet might become fatally damaged and out of balance. It is possible that a world war could destroy civilization and technology. Communications could disintegrate, and the few human survivors would be left fending for themselves in scattered communities across the globe.

Isolation begins

If Earth lost its technology, it could not communicate with its space colonies. Travel back and forth would become impossible. For people in space, life on Earth would become a memory, then a mythical story. The genes of the space travelers would become isolated and adapt to their new habitat. Over thousands of years, colonies on planets with strong gravity may become populated by people with stocky limbs, able to withstand the force; on those with weak gravity, the population may become tall and thin. Unique adaptations would be likely to occur.

New human species

If Earth eventually rebuilt its civilizations and its technology, it might send out emissaries to visit the colonies in space. The ambassadors would then find different humans, with new languages, strange body forms, and genes that could not intermingle with those of Earth's humans. New species of humans would thus form, and *Homo sapiens* would no longer be unique.

△ *In the past, when travel was slow and difficult, people found it easy to believe that people in distant countries were strange and monstrous. If planetary colonies became isolated, such beliefs could soon reappear. Such psychological isolation would add to the barriers between colonies.*

▷ *Humans on another planet would have new adaptations—perhaps an enlarged chest for coping with less oxygen, or larger eyes to let in more light. But the new humans would only be slightly different from us. It might be like looking at a reflection in a funhouse mirror.*

Alien Evolution

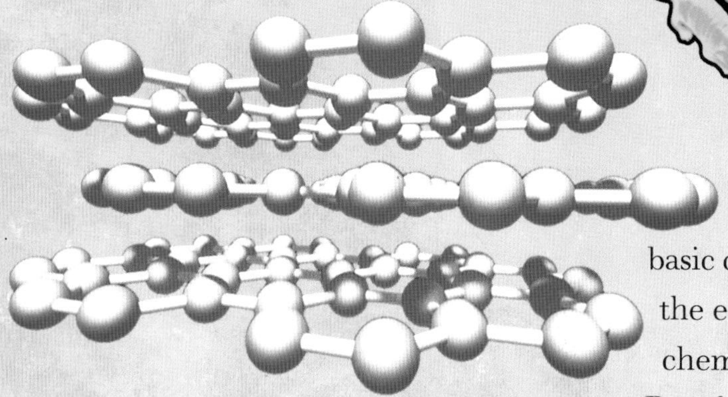

The theory of evolution states that life can start from simple beginnings. Energy is needed, as well as some basic chemicals. Three and a half billion years ago, conditions on the earth were right. The sun energized the earth, and life's chemicals leaked from the rocks, or rained out of the sky. But the universe is 14 billion years old, and these conditions have almost certainly existed on other, undiscovered planets. By now, life on these planets may be advanced. One day humans, or their descendants, may come in contact with alien life. And as the universe gets older, life may evolve into forms that humans can barely imagine now.

△ Carbon atoms, seen here joined together as graphite, are able to link with other kinds of atoms in many kinds of chains. This makes them ideal for constructing complex and diverse organic forms. Alien life might not be carbon-based, but it would need another element to fulfill the same role.

▽ This fictional colony of mucus-crystal symbionts have colonized a watery planet millions of years in the future. Their mucus bases collect food and make decisions. The crystals, being diamond-hard, are not harmed by the atmosphere. Their role is to reproduce and to beam information to one another.

Beyond carbon

Life on Earth is based on one vital chemical—carbon. This unusual atom can bond easily with other atoms. All the molecules that build the earth's organisms, such as proteins, are based on it. In fact, carbon-based life forms are so familiar to biologists that life based on a different element may not even be recognized. Yet all life is likely to have things in common. Even noncarbon life forms would have to be able to reproduce and sense the environment. Communication would also be vital.

Strange life forms

The new symbiotic organisms, or symbionts, would at first sight have almost nothing in common with life on Earth. Perhaps they would be able to travel vast distances across space. Because space travel is so time-consuming, they would have to be long-lived. Their bodies would degrade slowly and would have to be able to withstand the intense radiation of space. But as living things, they would also be able to reproduce and pass information to the next generation. So, how might these creatures look?

△ *However life evolves, healthy ecosystems require a diversity of life. On Earth, this is displayed best in the fertile rain forests.*

◁ *Human intelligence is only one by-product of evolution on Earth. There is no guarantee that alien evolution would create anything similar.*

Beyond the solar system

In a few billion years, life on Earth will end. The sun will expand, burning up all the planets. Whatever evolution has produced on Earth—*Homo sapiens* will be long extinct—its future will depend on escaping into the galaxy. Perhaps they will encounter other life forms. If Earth's carbon life meets alien life, the different life forms may merge or exchange material to be better adapted. This symbiosis, or "living together," would create organisms that owed something to Earth and something to aliens.

Life goes on

Perhaps the new life forms will be similar to crystals, attached to sheets of sticky, glutinous mucus. The crystal part is long-lasting and can seed new individuals. But the mucus base, being liquid, can run chemical reactions, organize communication, and think about the future. It is impossible to know. One thing is certain, however. As long as life in the universe exists, it will adapt to available habitats and will continue to evolve. And as long as it does that, the wondrous variety of life will be unending.

Evolution Facts

CLASSIFICATION OF LIVING THINGS

Life is divided into three main areas, or *domains*. The first two domains, **Bacteria** and **Archaea**, are made up of many microscopic, single-celled organisms. The third domain, **Eukarya**, is diverse and includes Protists, Fungi, Plants, and Animals. These groups are called *kingdoms*.

Kingdoms are subdivided into subgroups. These are:
Phylum—Organisms built to the same underlying plan.
Class—Part of a phylum. Contains organisms that share important features.
Order—Part of a class. Organisms in an order are usually similar in shape.
Family—Part of an order. Organisms in a family have similar ways of life.
Genus—Part of a family. A number of different species that are very closely related.
Species—A group of organisms that can breed together.

Every species has a Latin name that gives its genus and then its species name. This locates it exactly in the tree of life.

THE KINGDOMS OF EUKARYA

Protists
These are advanced single-celled organisms. Some behave like animals. Others are more like plants.

Fungi
These feed on living things or their dead remains and grow tiny threads that spread through their food. Most are microscopic; some grow toadstools when they reproduce.

Plants
Plants are multicellular organisms that capture the sun's energy to make the materials for life. Major groups of plants include green algae, seaweeds, primitive land plants such as liverworts and mosses, and vascular plants. **Vascular plants** can draw water up through their stems and are well suited to life on land. They include club mosses, horsetails, ferns, and seed plants. Seed plants are divided into *gymnosperms*, which produce uncovered seeds, and *angiosperms*, which produce flowers, fruit, and seeds enclosed in a protective seed case. Over half the species of plants in the world are angiosperms.

Animals
These are multicellular organisms that eat food to survive. Animals are varied. Their phyla include:
Cnidaria Animals with baglike bodies and stinging tentacles. Includes jellyfish, sea anemones, and corals.
Platyhelminthes Flatworms, or animals with paper-thin bodies. Most live in water or in other animals.
Annelids Segmented worms, including earthworms. They live in soil or water.
Mollusks Animals with soft bodies, often protected by a shell. Most live in water. They include snails and octopuses.
Echinoderms Sea animals with bodies divided into five identical parts. They include starfish and sea urchins.
Arthropods A hugely successful phylum of animals covered by a body case, or exoskeleton. They have several pairs of rigid, jointed legs. Subphyla include:
>*Crustaceans* Arthropods with two pairs of antennae. They include crabs, lobsters, and woodlice.
>*Chelicerates* These have a body divided into two parts. They do not have antennae. They include arachnids (spiders, scorpions, and ticks).
>*Uniramians* Arthropods with a single pair of antennae and unbranched legs. Includes two classes:
>>*Centipedes and millipedes* Long-bodied arthropods with many pairs of legs.
>>*Insects* The most numerous class. These have three pairs of legs and often two pairs of wings.

Chordates Animals with a reinforcing rod (notochord) running down their bodies. Subphlya include:
>*Cephalochordates* Chordates without a backbone that live in water. Includes lancelets.
>*Vertebrates* Chordates with a backbone and an internal skeleton. Vertebrates include these classes:
>>*Jawless fish* Fish with eellike bodies and no jaw.
>>*Cartilaginous fish* Fish with skeletons made of cartilage. Includes sharks and rays.
>>*Bony fish* Fish with bony skeletons and scaly skin. The most numerous of all vertebrates.
>>*Amphibians* Animals that live partly on land and partly in water. Includes frogs, toads, and newts.
>>*Reptiles* Animals with a scaly skin, living on land or water. Most lay eggs.
>>*Birds* Warm-blooded animals with wings, beaks, and feathers. Most can fly. All lay eggs.
>>*Mammals* Warm-blooded animals with fur or hair that feed their young milk.

GEOLOGICAL TIMELINE

m.y.a. = millions of years ago. The dates on the left indicate when each period begins.

m.y.a.	Period	Events
4,500	**Pre-Cambrian**	Formation of Earth
	(3,500 m.y.a.)	Oldest-known single-celled organisms
	(600 m.y.a.)	Oldest fossil animals and plants
570	**Cambrian**	First mollusks
		First chordates
500	**Ordovician**	First jawless fish
		First land-based plants
430	**Silurian**	First fish with jaws
		First land animals (invertebrates)
395	**Devonian**	First bony fish
		Vertebrates on land
345	**Carboniferous**	Great forests
		Many amphibians
		First reptiles
280	**Permian**	Mammallike reptiles are dominant
		Major extinction of marine creatures
225	**Triassic**	First dinosaurs
		First mammals
		Mammallike reptiles die out
190	**Jurassic**	Dinosaurs dominant
		First birds
136	**Cretaceous**	First flowering plants
	(66 m.y.a.)	Dinosaurs become extinct
65	**Tertiary**	The age of mammals
	Paleocene Epoch	Giant land birds
57	Eocene Epoch	First horses, whales
36	Oligocene Epoch	Grasslands spread
		Many grazing animals
23	Miocene Epoch	First ape
5	Pliocene Epoch	First upright apes
1.8	**Quaternary**	The age of humans
	Pleistocene Epoch	The Ice Age
		Development of modern humans
10,000 y.a.	Holocene Epoch	Modern civilizations

HISTORICAL TIMELINE

1735	Carl Linnaeus publishes *The System of Nature*. Introduces system of classification for plants and animals, including the concept of species.
1790s	A French zoologist, Georges Cuvier (1769–1832), begins the science of comparative anatomy. He compares the structure of animals' bodies. This allows similarities to be recorded, and is useful in establishing the nature of fossil remains.
1796	Cuvier reconstructs a *Megatherium*, a giant ground sloth found in South America.
1799	Alexander von Humboldt explores South America and brings back many new specimens.
1809	Lamarck publishes his theory of evolution.
1819	William Smith (1769–1839), a canal engineer, produces a geological map of England and Wales. He is the first to realize that different layers of rock (strata) contain different kinds of fossils.
1830	Sir Charles Lyell publishes his *Principles of Geology*, providing proof that the world is much older than previously thought.
1831	Charles Darwin sets sail on board the *Beagle*.
1842	Richard Owen (1804–1892), professor of anatomy in London, determines many fossils are from an extinct group of reptiles. He names them dinosaurs—"terrible lizards."
1856	Neanderthal bones are discovered in a German quarry. Many scientists believe they belong to a diseased modern human.
1858	Alfred Russel Wallace sends Darwin the details of his evolutionary theory. Darwin and Wallace publish a joint paper outlining their ideas.
1859	Darwin publishes *The Origin of Species*.
1860	The first fossilized *Archaeopteryx* is discovered. It is the first example of a transition between two major classes of animals.
1860s	Gregor Mendel conducts experiments on garden peas. These provide evidence for inheritance, but his work is not widely recognized until 1900.
1885	German naturalist August Weismann (1834–1914) investigates inheritance. He realizes the nucleus of sex cells carries genetic information.
1924	First australopithecine fossil, a skull nicknamed the "Taung child," is found in South Africa.
1953	Watson and Crick discover the structure of DNA.
1997	A sheep named Dolly is the first mammal to be cloned from an adult cell.
2000	Research into the code for the human genome nears completion.

Glossary

Adaptation A change in the structure or behavior of an organism that makes it better able to live in a particular environment.

Altruism Any behavior by an individual organism that benefits others at the individual's own expense.

Amino acid One of twenty molecules that join together to make protein molecules. Their sequence is determined by the DNA's genetic code.

Arthropod An animal with a hard, protective exoskeleton and several pairs of jointed legs. Arthropods include lobsters, spiders, and insects.

Asexual reproduction The production of offspring in which genetic material from only one individual is used.

Atom The smallest particle of matter. Atoms are made from a variety of elements. The carbon atom is a vital component of all organic structures.

Base One of four molecules—adenine, thymine, guanine, and cytosine—that form the linking structures in the DNA spiral. The sequence of the bases forms the organism's essential genetic code.

Bipedal Capable of standing, walking, and running on two legs.

Carnivore Any animal or plant that eats the flesh of animals.

Cell A unit of living matter, surrounded by a membrane. The smallest living things are single cells. Many organisms are multicellular, with different cells adapted to different tasks.

Characteristic A specific quality in the behavior or body structure of an organism. Many characteristics are under genetic control and can be inherited.

Chromosome A structure in a cell's nucleus that contains the organism's DNA. In animal and plant cells, chromosomes exist in pairs, with one chromosome in each pair coming from each parent.

Clone An individual whose genetic makeup is identical to that of another individual.

Continental drift The theory that the earth's crust is divided into giant moving sections, or plates, which are propelled by heat rising from below. This makes the continents move in different directions over millions of years.

Convergent evolution The phenomenon in which distantly related animals evolve similar body plans in response to the same environmental pressures. For example, birds, bats, and pterosaurs all evolved sophisticated wings for flying.

Creationism The belief that everything that exists was created by God as described in Genesis. Creationists do not believe in evolution.

DNA (Deoxyribonucleic acid) The molecule inside the cells of all organisms that stores their genetic information. It is composed of two spiral strands linked by a sequence of chemical bases. The order of these bases forms the organism's genetic code.

Ecology The scientific study of plants, animals, and other organisms in relation to their environment.

Environment The place in which a population of organisms exists. It includes the climate, geology, and all neighboring plants and animals. Changes in the environment have a major effect on how a species evolves.

Evolution The gradual change in the physical traits of a species over time, resulting from genetic variation and natural selection, and leading to the appearance of new species.

Extinction The disappearance of an entire species. A species can also disappear by evolving into a new species. If many species become extinct at the same time, this is called a mass extinction. Mass extinctions have happened several times in the earth's history, such as at the end of the Permian Period (225 m.y.a.), when over 90 percent of all living things became extinct. The mass extinction at the end of the Cretaceous Period (65 m.y.a.) killed the dinosaurs and many other species.

Fertilization The fusing of a male and a female sex cell, making a fertilized cell. Their chromosomes combine, and a new organism develops.

Fossil The remains or imprint of an organism preserved in rock or another material, such as amber.

Gamete A sex cell made by a male or female to be used in fertilization. It contains half the usual number of chromosomes.

Gene A section of DNA that contains the information needed to create the structure of a single protein. Genes can be inherited and are passed from generation to generation.

Genetic modification The artificial alteration of an organism's genes by humans.

Genetic variation The small differences in the DNA code that make each individual organism unique.

Genetics The science of studying genes and inheritance.

Genome The total number of genes in a full set of chromosomes. The genome contains all of an individual's genetic information.

Genus A number of different species that are closely related to one another.

Geology The scientific study of the earth's crust, including its history, its strata (layers of rock), and the fossils it contains.

Germ-line therapy The replacing or doctoring of genes in a human sex cell. This can change the baby's genes and those of its descendants.

Herbivore An animal that eats only plants.

Heredity The transmission of characteristics or traits from one generation to the next.

Histones Proteins found in the cell nucleus. The DNA molecule coils around them in the chromosome.

Homeothermy "Warm-bloodedness"—the ability of some animals to keep their body temperature constantly warm. This allows the development of fast reactions and a quick, agile brain, but requires a constant supply of food. Mammals and birds are both homeothermic. Many scientists believe that some dinosaurs were probably homeothermic, too.

Hominid A member of the mammal family Hominidae, which includes *Homo sapiens*, our extinct ancestors, and modern gorillas and chimpanzees.

Inheritance The transfer of genetic information from one generation to the next.

Invertebrate Any animal that does not have a backbone. Invertebrates include many successful groups, such as mollusks, starfish, worms, and arthropods.

Meiosis An important kind of cell division that forms the male and female sex cells. During meiosis, the cell's chromosomes pair up and swap sections to create new genetic combinations. At the end of meiosis, the resulting sex cells, or gametes, have only half the usual number of chromosomes. They will regain the full number at the moment of fertilization.

Membrane A layer of molecules that forms the surface of cells and of many structures inside them. Membranes act as a barrier, allowing some chemicals in and keeping others out.

Microbe A microscopic organism, such as a bacterium.

Mitochondrion A structure in a cell that provides energy to help the cell function.

Molecule Two or more atoms linked together by chemical bonds. Molecules can be simple or very complex— like DNA, which is made of many millions of atoms.

Monogamy A sexual strategy in which an organism mates with only one partner during a mating season.

Mutation A change in the sequences of the bases in an organism's DNA. Mutations can be caused by radiation or toxic chemicals and can damage the organism. Only mutations that occur in the sex cells can be passed on to the next generation.

Natural selection The central process of evolution. Because of genetic variation, some individuals in a species will be more likely than others to survive in their environment and have more offspring. Their genetic characteristics will be passed on more often to the next generation than other combinations, and will increase in the population as a whole. In effect, the environment is "selecting" among the different genetic variations.

Neuron A cell that transmits nerve impulses in an animal's body. There are billions of neurons in the brain and spinal cord.

Notochord A supporting rod that runs along the body of all chordates.

Nucleus The central, controlling structure found inside every cell in animals, plants, or fungi. It contains the chromosomes.

Nutrient Any substance that gives an organism food or nourishment.

Organelle A structure inside a cell. Organelles have many different functions, and include mitochondria and ribosomes.

Organism A single living thing.

Parasite An organism that lives at the expense of an organism of another species. Parasites usually live on or in their host, and take nutrients from its body tissues.

Pheromone A chemical secreted by an animal that influences the behavior of others of its species. Many types of animals use pheromones to attract a mate.

Phylum A major grouping of organisms that have important characteristics in common.

Pollination The transfer of a plant's pollen to another plant, which it will fertilize. This is often done by insects, which carry the pollen on their bodies as they fly from plant to plant.

Polygamy A sexual strategy in which an organism mates with more than one partner in a mating season.

Population A group of individuals of the same species that live in a particular environment and that breed together.

Predator An animal that preys on another.

Primate An order of mammals, mostly tree-dwellers. Primates have flexible shoulder and elbow joints, highly mobile thumbs, big toes, and a large brain. The order includes lemurs, monkeys, apes, modern humans, and all extinct early humans.

Protein A molecule made from a sequence of amino acids. The sequence is coded by DNA. Proteins are vital for building the body's cells.

Radiation Energy in the form of rays. Strong doses of radiation can damage the body's structures, including DNA.

Reproduction The production of offspring by an organism. *See also* **Sexual reproduction** and **Asexual reproduction**.

Reproductive isolation A situation in which one group of animals of a particular species is isolated from other groups and is unable to breed with them. In time, genetic variation may turn the group into a new species.

Ribosome A tiny structure in a cell where the genetic code is read and used to manufacture proteins.

Sexual reproduction The creation of offspring by mixing the genetic information of two adult individuals. *See also* **Asexual reproduction**.

Special creation The belief that Earth and the living things that it contains were created by God all at once.

Speciation The formation of two new species from one. Often this happens when groups of a species are separated and evolve in slightly different ways.

Species A group of individual organisms that are able to interbreed.

Symbiosis A partnership between different kinds of organisms that is mutually beneficial.

Tectonic plates Giant sections of the earth's crust, which slowly move on its surface, propelled by the hot, liquid rocks underneath.

Theologian A specialist in the study of God and religion. In the past, they were also considered experts on how and why life formed.

Theory In science, an idea or explanation that can be put to the test by further experiments. Darwin's evolutionary theory has been tested many times, and after nearly 150 years, it still fits the observable facts.

Vertebrate Any animal with a backbone. Vertebrate species include fish, amphibians, reptiles, birds, and mammals, including humans.

Zygote The fertilized cell produced by the union of the male and female gametes. The zygote quickly begins to develop into a new organism.

Index

Acknowledgments

The publishers would like to thank the following illustrators: **James Field** 38–39, 40–41, 42–43, 44–45, 46–47, 48–49, 50–51, 68–69, 70–71, 72–73, 74–75; **Gary Hincks** 9 *bl, tr*, 11 *cl*, 14 *br*, 17 *br*, 22–23 *c, tr*, 24–25 *c*, 30–31 *b*, 44–45 *cr, bl*, 52 *l*, 63 *br*, 67, 69 *br*, 73 *br*; **Mark Preston** (*digital montages*) 6–7, 78–79, 80–81, 88–89; **Steve Rawlings** 8–9, 10–11, 12–13, 16–17, 18–19, 20–21, 26 *c*, 82–83, 84–85, 86–87, (*digital montages and icons*) **Guy Smith** 52–53, 81 *cl*, **Holly Warburton** Cover, 14–15 (*digital montages*).

The publishers would like to thank the following for supplying photographs:

Front cover *bc* NHPA, *cl* The Natural History Museum, London, *cr* Science Photo Library/Astrid and Hanns-Frieder Michler, *c* The Natural History Museum, London, *tl* Science Photo Library/John Reader, *cl* Planet Earth Pictures/K. and K. Ammann, *bl* The Natural History Museum, London, *t* NHPA/ Dr. Eckart Pott, *br* Planet Earth Pictures/Mark Schumann; **Back cover** *cl* Planet Earth Pictures/Geoff du Feu, *tl* Science Photo Library/John Reader; **Endpapers** AKG London.

4-5 *t* Science Photo Library/Astrid and Hanns-Frieder Michler, **5** *cr* Science Photo Library/John Reader, *br* Science Photo Library/Makoto Iwafuji, **6** *tl* Planet Earth Pictures/ Beth Davidow, *cr* NHPA/Martin Harvey, **8** *tr* The Natural History Museum, London, **9** *cr* The Art Archive/Museo Nazionale, Rome, **10** *tl* The Art Archive/ Gemaldgalerie, Dresden, *br* The Bridgeman Art Library/ British Library, London, **11** *tr* The Art Archive/British Library, London, *bc* Hulton Getty, **12-13** *bc* AKG London/Akademie der Wissenschaften, Berlin, **13** *tl* Jean-Loup Charmet *cr* The Bridgeman Art Library/Natural History Museum, London, *br* The Art Archive/Gallerie Borghese, Rome, **14** *tr* Jean-Loup Charmet, **15** *tr* The Natural History Museum, London, *cl* English Heritage Photographic Library, *c* English Heritage Photographic Library, *cr* The Bridgeman Art Library/Harriet Wynter Antiques, London, *br* Geoscience Features Picture Library, **16** *tr* Mary Evans Picture Library, *bl* BBC Photographic library, *br* Planet Earth Pictures/Ken Lucas, **17** *tc* The Natural History Museum, London, **18** *tl* Mary Evans Picture Library, *bl* Mary Evans Picture Library, *br* Mary Evans Picture Library, **19** *tl* The Bridgeman Art Library/ Down House, Downe, Kent, *tr* Science Photo Library, *c* The Bridgeman Art Library/Natural History Museum, London, *br* Mary Evans Picture Library, **20** *bl* Science Photo Library/ A. Barrington Brown, *br* The Ronald Grant Archive, **21** *tl* Science Photo Library/Simon Fraser, *cl* Mary Evans Picture Library, *cr* The Ronald Grant Archive, *br* The Ronald Grant Archive, **22** *cl* Science Photo Library/Dept of Clinical Cytogenetics, Addenbrookes Hospital, Cambridge, *bl* Science Photo Library/Dr. Gopal Murti, **23** *b* Science Photo Library/ Prof. K. Seddon and Dr. T. Evans, Queen's Universtiy, Belfast, **24** *tl* Science Photo Library, *bl* Science Photo Library/ D. Philips, **25** *tr* Tony Stone Images/Bob Thomas, *c* NHPA/ G. I. Bernard, *b* Planet Earth Pictures/Jonathan Scott, **26** *tr* Planet Earth Pictures/Georgette Douwma, *bl* Science Photo Library/David Scharf, **27** *tr* Science Photo Library/ Martin Dohrn, *c* NHPA/Laurie Campbell, *bl* The Bridgeman Art Library/Central Saint Martins College of Art and Design, **28** *tl* Oxford Scientific Films/Densey Clyne, *bl* Oxford Scientific Films/David Cayless, *br* NHPA/Daryl Balfour, **29** *tr* NHPA/Stephen Dalton, *b* Planet Earth Pictures/Frank Krahmer, **30** *tl* NHPA/Dave Watts, **30-31** (*background image*) Geoscience Features Picture Library, **31** *tl* Oxford Scientific Films/Dr. F. Koster, *tc* NHPA/Kevin Schafer, *tr* Oxford Scientific Films/Dieter and Mary Plage, **32** *tr* Oxford Scientific Films/Satoshi Kuribayashi, *cl* NHPA/M.I. Walker, *br* Planet Earth Pictures/Geoff du Feu, **33** *tr* Oxford Scientific Films/Zig Leszczysnki, *cl* Frank Lane Picture Agency/ S.Vannini/ Panda, *br* NHPA/Daniel Heuclin, **34** *tl* Science Photo Library, **35** *tl* Science Photo Library/Alfred Pasieka, *cl* The Natural History Museum, London, *cr* Planet Earth Pictures/Peter Scoones, **36** *tc* Science Photo Library/David Parker, *bl* Science Photo Library/Eye of Science, **37** *tr* Science Photo Library/ Professors P. Motta and T. Naguro, *c* Science Photo Library/D. A. Peel, *bl* Mary Evans Picture Library, *br* NHPA/Stephen Dalton, **38** *tr* Science Photo Library/Detlev van Ravenswaay, *cl* NHPA/Image Quest 3-D, *br* Science Photo Library, **39** *tr* Science Photo Library/B. Murton/Southampton Oceanography Centre, **40** *tl* The Natural History Museum, London, *c* Corbis, **41** *tl* Geoscience Features Picture Library, *c* Frank Lane Picture Agency/David Hosking, **42** *c* Frank Lane Picture Agency/ Peter Reynolds, *br* Bruce Coleman Collection/John Shaw, **43** *t* Bruce Coleman Collection/MPL Fogden, **44** *tl* Dr. Mike Coates, *br* Oxford Scientific Films/Fran Allan/Animals Animals, **45** *cr* Planet Earth Pictures/Ken Lucas, **46** *tr* Ardea London/Francois Gohier, *cl* Ardea London/Francoise Gohier, **47** *tr* The Natural History Museum, London, **48** *bl* Geoscience Features Picture Library, **49** *tl* Planet Earth Pictures/Richard Matthews, *c* Oxford Scientific Films/Mike Birkhead, *br* NHPA/Paal Hemansen, **51** *tr* Planet Earth Pictures/Tom Brakefield, *cr* Planet Earth Pictures/Nick Greaves, **54** *tl* Still Pictures/Fred Bruemmer, *bl* Warren Photographic, **55** *tl* Ardea London/M.W. Gillam, *bc* Oxford Scientific Films/Raymond Mendez, **56** *tl* NHPA/Bruce Beehler, *c* Warren Photographic/ Jane Burton, *b* Ardea London/Jack A. Bailey, **57** *t* Oxford Scientific Films/John Mitchell, *c* Oxford Scientific Films/Rudie H Kuiter, *b* Oxford Scientific Films, **58** *t* NHPA/Stephen Dalton, *c* Science Photo Library/Dr. Tony Brain, *br* NHPA/Agence Nature, **59** *t* Oxford Scientific Films/Densey Clyne, *b* NHPA Peter Pickford, **60** *tr* Planet Earth Pictures/Chris Huxley, *cr* Frank Lane Picture Agency/D. T. Grewcock, **61** *tl* NHPA/Daniel Heuclin, *tr* Planet Earth Pictures/Jonathan Scott, *cl* Oxford Scientific Films/ Rodger Jackman, *br* Planet Earth Pictures/Tom Arnbom, **62** *tl* Frank Lane Picture Agency/R. Austing, *cr* Bruce Coleman Collection/Gunter Ziesler, *bl* Planet Earth Pictures/Georgette Douwma, **63** *tl* Ardea London/Francois Gohier, *c* Warren Photographic/Mark Taylor, **64** *tr* Planet Earth Pictures/Geoff du Feu, *c* Frank Lane Picture Agency/ Gerard Lacz, *br* Oxford Scientific Films/J & B Photographers, **65** *tr* NHPA/Dr. Ivan Polunin, *cl* Tony Stone Images/Art Wolfe, *br* Planet Earth Pictures/K. and K. Ammann, **66** *tl* Science Photo Library/ CNRI, *tc* Science Photo Library/John Reader, *c* Tony Stone Images/Kevin Anderson, *cr* Tony Stone Images/Robert Van Der Hilst, *bl* Planet Earth Pictures/Terry Mayes, *bc* Bubbles Photolibrary/Jennie Woodcock, (*background picture*) Tony Stone Images/Andrew Errington, **68** *t* Oxford Scientific Films/ Matthew/Purdy, *c* Science Photo Library/John Reader, **69** *t* Science Photo Library/John Reader, **70** *tl* Science Photo Library/John Reader, *tr* Science Photo Library/John Reader, *b* Michael Holford, *tl* Science Photo Library/John Reader, **72** *tl* C. M. Dixon, **73** *tl* C. M. Dixon, *c* NHPA/Stephen Krasemann, **74** *tc* C. M. Dixon, *cl* Science Photo Library/John Reader, *br* The Natural History Museum, London, *tl* Science Photo Library/John Reader, **76** *tl* Tony Stone Images/Demetrio Carrasco, *cr* Michael Holford, *bc* Tony Stone Images/Yann Layma, **76-77** (*background picture*) Ancient Art and Architecture, **77** *tl* Tony Stone Images/Chad Ehlers, *c* Tony Stone Images/Wayne Eastep, *br* Science Photo Library/ Sam Ogden, **78** *tl* Science Photo Library/Makoto Iwafuji/ Eurelios, *tr* Science Photo Library/L.Willatt/East Anglian Regional Genetics Service, *bl* Science Photo Library/Peter Menzel, **79** *cl* Science Photo Library/C. C. Studio, *c* Science Photo Library/ Makoto Iwafuji, **80** *tl* Science Photo Library/ Klaus Guldbrandsen, *tc* Science Photo Library/Makoto Iwafuji, *cl* Science Photo Library/David Mooney, **81** *br* PPL Therapeutics, **82** *t* Science Photo Library/Makoto Iwafuji, *tl* Environmental Images/Martin Bond, *cl* Ardea London/A. Greensmith, *bl* Environmental Images/Herbert Girardet, *br* Sharna Balfour; Gallow Images/Corbis, **83** *tl* Science Photo Library/ Dr. Karl Lounatmaa, *cr* Robert Harding Picture Library/ C. Bowman, *bl* Still Pictures, *br* Oxford Scientific Films/ Ronald Toms, **84** *tl* Science Photo Library/ Makoto Iwafuji, *br* Oxford Scientific Films/Mark Deeble and Victoria Stone, **85** *tl* Tony Stone Images/Jerry Alexander, **86** *tl* Science Photo Library/Makoto Iwafuji, *tr* Science Photo Library/ NASA, *bl* Tony Stone Images/Bob Thomas, **87** *tr* The Art Archive/Bibliotheque Nationale, Paris, **88** *tl* Science Photo Library/Ken Eward, *tc* Science Photo Library/Makoto Iwafuji, **89** *tl* Oxford Scientific Films/Ronald Toms, *tc* Tony Stone Images/Phillip and Karen Smith.

Key: b = bottom, c = center, l = left, r = right, t= top
Every effort has been made to trace the copyright holders of the photographs. The publishers apologize for any inconvenience caused.

The publishers would also like to thank Dr. Mike Coates.